Inclusion Around The Clock

Celebrating Diversity & Inclusion with Pluribus

ISABELLE PUJOL

and 12 authors from the Pluribus Global Network

Inclusion Around The Clock

First published in 2016 by

Panoma Press Ltd,
48 St Vincent Drive, St Albans, Herts, AL1 5SJ, UK
info@panomapress.com
www.panomapress.com

Book layout by Neil Coe.

Printed on acid-free paper from managed forests.

ISBN 978-1-784521-01-1

Dedication

This book is dedicated to all our families, children, friends, Pluribus facilitators, colleagues, mentors and clients from all over the globe who have the courage and the willingness to be a strong force for positive change in the world. We need you as you are leading the way by "walking the talk" and inspiring us for more inclusion around us!

"I wonder," he said "whether the stars are set alight
in heaven
so that one day each one of us may find his own
again."

Antoine de Saint-Exupéry - The Little Prince

Contents

Foreword

by Rohini Anand

Close to ten years ago, I had the pleasure of meeting Isabelle Pujol while attending a global diversity conference in Berlin. At that time Pluribus was just getting started and was in its very early phases of evolving into the strategic consulting partner that it has become today. From the very beginning Isabelle and I connected and I knew immediately that, based on our common interest in advancing global diversity and inclusion, the likelihood of a partnership was inevitable. At the time there were not as many diversity consultants in Europe, and certainly not many who truly embraced the issues across all the dimensions, with their nuances and complexities, and were able to facilitate constructive dialogue on the topic. Sodexo needed assistance in raising awareness on the topic and facilitating a conversation in a non-threatening way. Isabelle and Pluribus were the perfect choice!

Shortly thereafter, we hosted a Global Women's Summit and a Global Inclusion Summit with the senior leaders across Sodexo and Isabelle facilitated an exceptional session on gender and unconscious bias, which was very well received. Isabelle's ability to articulate concepts clearly and simply, along with her authenticity, completely aligned with Sodexo's culture. Given the initial success, Sodexo and Pluribus continued to partner on the design and delivery of our Spirit of Inclusion workshop, which was successfully rolled out in most of our European regions, engaging our leadership teams and identifying Diversity & Inclusion champions through the Train the Trainer process. Since then, Pluribus has been involved in supporting Sodexo in additional regions, including the Middle East, and has remained a valued partner in our diversity and inclusion journey.

The Sodexo/Pluribus partnership is not your typical vendor/client relationship, but rather a collaborative commitment to creating, learning and growing together; a commitment that has allowed me to witness and be a part of the global growth and success that Pluribus has achieved over the past ten years, and that I'm sure will continue for many years to come.

So, as Pluribus celebrates this ten year milestone, I want to personally thank you, Isabelle, not only for your leadership, but for your support in Sodexo's journey, and your commitment to helping individuals, teams and organizations succeed, through diversity and inclusion. I wish you and the Pluribus team continued success and look forward to our continued partnership.

Sincerely

Rohini Anand, Ph.D.
Senior Vice President Corporate Responsibility &
Global Chief Diversity Officer
Sodexo

Introduction

by Isabelle Pujol, Founder and Director of Pluribus

"Many seek illumination by lighting a lamp when the true light is within our heart."

Shi Cheng Yen

Every project and act of creation, such as painting, having a baby or founding a consulting business like Pluribus, begins with the not-knowing, unconsciousness and being in the dark.

I would like to honor the model of the Creative Process which has been my personal golden thread over the last ten years. I came across this model when I left BP and it led me in the next phases of my life. This model is based on the very old four-part archetypes of the primary elements and what they symbolize:

Water for stillness – After more than 20 years in the corporate world as an employee, I needed to reflect about what was going to emerge for me. It all started by openly listening to my inner voice, by pausing and quietening down. I had to resist the urge to move on too quickly.

Air for connection – After this time for myself, I was able to be open to exploring the field of possibilities. I had multiple conversations with diverse people to share and listen to new thoughts and ideas. Soon, opportunities were showing up while I continued to hold back the impulse to act.

Earth for action – Pluribus was born in November 2006. I developed a plan and determined what needed to be done. I was aware of the accelerating momentum and saw Pluribus growing from a local to a global reach, supported by a wonderful and talented team of Diversity & Inclusion practitioners. Strategic conversations, design works, speeches, consultings, facilitation – lot of involvement and actions.

Fire for results – As Pluribus continues to unfold and the results show up, there is a sense of recognition and achievement and even a life of its own. It is time for celebration!

1. Why has this book been written now?

Today is indeed about celebration. The fire and the joy!

Pluribus is turning ten years old and writing this collective book was the option we selected to stop, reflect and celebrate ten years of learnings, discoveries and adventures. This book is for you! Ten years of inspiration, co-creation, sharing, growing and learning together, creativity, energy and true care. Thank you! This book is celebrating what we have accomplished *together*, the visible and invisible stakeholders of the Pluribus system: our clients, supporters, colleagues, mentors, families and friends. I, as a person, or we at Pluribus, learned so much on the ongoing journey. Navigating through the invisible field of the creative process has been a beautiful adventure. Small achievements, probably minor steps in our respective spheres of influence. And I strongly believe in small steps.

I feel a lot of gratitude for all the clients who trusted us and everyone who helped us along the journey. Merci!

And a deep thank you to the culturally diverse contributors (Pluribus Associates and Pluribus friends from nine different nationalities: American, French, English, Spanish, Dutch, Belgian, Swiss, Argentinean and Turkish) for your respective insights, ideas and passions on the various topics. We selected the English language to write this book to make it global and more accessible.

2. Who is this book intended for and why?

Anyone who is interested in the topic of Diversity & Inclusion can read this book, whatever gender, age, culture or background. We worked collectively to write diverse chapters that were meaningful to every one of us. *Inclusion Around The Clock* is a collection of stories based on personal anecdotes or pieces of research from various Pluribus facilitators or people with a strong connection to Pluribus. We hope it will give you insights, different views, some reassurances or maybe some surprises on various topics related to creating and building inclusive environments that value all facets of diversity.

Inclusion Around The Clock is *not* a Diversity & Inclusion "bible" with "to-do-lists," answers or toolkits. There are hundreds of great books already in the market which can provide this.

3. How can you read this book?

You can pick the chapters that you are most interested in rather than reading it from end to end. Just enjoy the different pieces, different styles, different stories. Ultimately, the book is an invitation to spark your interest and engagement in various facets of inclusion. Join us in playing an active role in promoting a more inclusive and diverse world where everyone can feel valued, listened to and respected. The world we live in and all of us need this!

Genesis of Pluribus

by Isabelle Pujol

1. Reflecting into my personal connections to Diversity & Inclusion

Experiencing feeling different

I can't talk about my personal connection to diversity and inclusion without referring to the story of my parents. My parents were respectively 28 and 20 when they moved to Paris in 1962 from Tunis. It was not their decision. It was a question of survival. They left while the North African countries asked for their independence. My father's brother already lived in Paris so it was natural that they would move to the capital city despite their love for the Mediterranean sea and the warm weather. They had to start from scratch. They immediately faced a cultural shock. Everything was different: the food, the environment, the work, the relationship between people, the religion. Their accent was different despite a French education in Tunis. They were different. They felt different.

And then I was born in 1963 in Paris, the eldest of four children. I only remember being loved and cared for, especially as the first child and first grandchild. Every weekend would be spent with my grandparents, cousins, our Jewish community. Always something to celebrate and eat! So many beautiful memories of endless meals with families and friends. And yet, my parents were very protective, probably because they did not feel part of the larger French community. It is only at the age of ten that I personally felt I was also different.

This took me by surprise one day at school. I was in the 5th grade and everyone was excited about the first ski trip organized by the school. Imagine, four weeks in Savoie with my friends. And yet, I knew that my parents did not have a lot of money. Only my father was working. My mother was committed to raising her children in a very traditional way, totally devoted to her children. My dad was the HR manager of a BTP company dealing with a lot of North African employees as he also spoke Arabic. I could feel that money was an issue at home even though we never lacked anything, including going to the Côte d'Azur every summer! So one day, while I was in the classroom with my teacher and the other children, my father came to the classroom, asking for a short discussion with the teacher. I will always remember the impression of discomfort I felt that day. Even though no one else noticed the reason why he came to the classroom, I knew that he was asking for an arrangement for paying the fee of the ski trip. I felt different and it took me days to smile again. I don't know whether I was experiencing for the first time the dynamics of excluding myself but this is what I did. I just wanted to be invisible. No doubt that my performance at school decreased the first few days and then I suddenly realized that it was not right so I reacted. I found some inner strength to be visible and to own who I was.

Experiencing cultural diversity

While I was organizing my student exchange program in California after my degree in high school, I did not expect that this trip would play such a central role in my life. Despite several European trips with my parents, this was the first time I was traveling outside Europe. I was 18 and eager to live different adventures. I found myself in an American movie, California's dreams! My hosting family was so wonderful. I felt included and welcomed the minute I met them. I felt so free to discover, to explore, to share, to learn. For me, this period gave me the foundations for building a respectful curiosity for cultural diversity: ask questions, clarify, communicate, laugh. I will always keep the beautiful memory of meeting my American family who opened their arms and their hearts to me. We will soon celebrate 34 years of close friendship and real love. As my American sister would say, "Our friends are the family we choose." I have a lot of gratitude for this precious relationship I keep for every member of my American family.

This first trip marked the stone for so many trips around the world. Up to today, I have a big world map offered by my children where I would put a pin for each location visited across the globe. All these different colorful dots/pins mark a place on a colorful world map and bring alive the tastes, the cultures, the music, the colleagues, the friends, the clients and the memories of shared experiences. They nurse my work on inclusion.

Experiencing different working environments

The restaurant

I often tell people that when I started my career in the corporate world, my husband Jean-Marc who was in the hotel/restaurant business asked me to help him fulfill his dream: to open a restaurant with him. I stopped everything to support him and the adventure of owning and running a restaurant lasted two years. It was hard work and this was the first experience of self-entrepreneurship. But at this time, it did not occur to me that I was an entrepreneur. I was just following my husband and did my best to fulfill his expectations. Step by step, I enjoyed the freedom of being my own boss, despite the fact that, from time to time, I had the feeling my husband was my boss! My love for connection with people, for creating an inclusive and friendly atmosphere in the restaurant, helped with diving into a world I was not aware of. The 24/7 approach of running a restaurant helped me immensely when I joined BP in France.

The oil industry

I started with joining the communication and the press office team. The role was junior but my asset was to be fluent in English. The global headquarters being based in the U.K., a lot of the tasks were dealing with managers and journalists in London. Step by step, I was able to prove myself and to be part of exciting projects. Less than a year later, I was offered the chance to move to Brussels, at the European headquarters, as a full expatriate. I know that my boss thought I was going to refuse the job as I was married and already had a three-year-old son, Raphael. The assumption that the woman would stay where the husband works was strong. In fact, it became very clear that moving to Brussels was the right thing to do. A lot of people did not take the opportunity because there was no guarantee to have a job after two years in Belgium. We were up for the opportunity and the risk. These two years became eight years – eight years of development and learning possibilities. Great colleagues and great mentors who saw my potential, my curiosity, my passion and my willingness to stretch my limits. I have so much gratitude for them. They will recognize themselves!

"One day, you will wake up and there won't be any more time

to do the things you've always wanted. Do it now."

Paulo Coelho

Female expatriate

When I was pregnant with my second child Sarah, I became the first woman expat pregnant within BP in Europe. I remember the HR office telling me that during my maternity leave I would lose my expatriation package. I was shocked by this and replied right away whether anyone with a broken leg and on sick leave would lose their expatriation package. Of course this scenario had never happened before. So after a few conversations it became clear that I would keep my expatriation package. I was able to speak up, to raise my voice and I was heard. Sometimes we don't dare ask and we feel frustrated because we don't share our feelings and because we feel we are not seen. I wanted to be responsible for not excluding myself and I raised my concerns. At that time BP was going through a major process of mergers and acquisitions and truly wanted to become a progressive and global organization. It became very obvious that the Diversity & Inclusion topic was becoming a strategic issue. I was pregnant with Sarah when I was asked to lead a task force on the gender topic to understand why there were so few women as part of the European leadership team and especially to understand the challenges faced by women. I was appointed the first chair of the European Women's Network back in 1992. I met incredible women from all over Europe and we initiated a lot of projects like mentoring and job shadowing programs to encourage women to speak up and explore new job opportunities. I was then promoted to move to the worldwide head office and take up the first full-time global role on Diversity & Inclusion in 1998. Everyone was looking at me asking themselves what this role could be.

Diving into the D&I topic within BP

I felt very lonely on various occasions, especially being the only woman in many meetings. This was a beautiful and yet challenging experience dealing with senior managers in the UK.

One day, I had an important presentation to make in front of a very senior group of executives at the global head office in London in the main boardroom. I remember when I started to say "bonjour" in French. Everybody was surprised but politely smiled back at me. Their smiles quickly became a grimace when I carried on in French. For nearly 15 seconds, they could not imagine what was going on. They started to feel uncomfortable, moved their chairs. Of course, I switched back to English. I was terrified and I was trembling. Yet, I was able to make my point. "You are all English or American here, I am French. I need to make an effort to speak in English. You might take this for granted. I am a woman. You are all men here. I feel in the minority, different. You are all very senior, the cream of the cream. I am relatively junior. So I am here to present to you the first Diversity & Inclusion strategy which is to focus on how to ensure that we can leverage the diversity of all our people. And now, I feel so different that I am losing my confidence." This is when I paused. Everybody was watching me. I remember when the CEO at that time said, "We heard you, please make your presentation." I did it. Then at the end of the presentation, everyone stood up and came to me to shake my hand. "You made your point. Thank you for raising our awareness."

Here again, how many times we don't express ourselves when we feel excluded or different. I was able to speak up, shared my feelings and vulnerability. This was my strength and it worked.

2. Searching for my personal calling

Listening to my body

After a number of years of traveling, working really hard in various exciting projects across the world, I felt miserable. I felt guilty because of this feeling. How could I feel this way when I had a family and a job? And yet, my body was sending me signs. Strong signs. Repetitive bronchitis. Regular pains in my bones. I was not happy anymore. I could not get up in the morning with a smile. I was having panic attacks each time I was flying out, and at that time I had at least one or two flights every week. I was becoming very down. I was 41 when this happened. I was a member of the Leadership Team of BP Oil in Germany and a member of the Advisory Board of BP Germany Marketing. I remember my naturopath telling me that I had to radically change the way I was leading my life otherwise something serious could happen to my health. I don't know why I took him seriously. For six weeks, I stayed at home on sick leave. I could not relax. I could not sleep. I knew I had to make a radical decision.

Coming into my own

You can spend your whole life trying to answer the fundamental question from Mary Oliver's *Summer Day*: "What will you do with your one wild and precious life?" and yet not be sure with the answers. I was fortunate to cross the path of several women who really inspired me. They gave me the opportunity to attend a magical program called "Coming into Your Own."

This is actually more than just a program. My first experience as a participant was like an eye-opening moment. This was probably the first time I could just stop and think about who I really wanted to be. Talking about your calling requires listening from the heart and sensing deeply what is unique about what you do, who you are and how you want to express yourself in the world. Throughout the program, I liked the fact that I had to acknowledge my past especially with the lens of the important turning points, then to think about my present and my current challenges. Then I was able to think about the future I really wanted. The approach was very transformational as it touched not only my mind and my heart but also my body and my connection with nature. I was able to reflect, explore and regenerate, and meet other beautiful and inspiring women. The wisdom of women from various horizons, worlds, generations, backgrounds. All wanted to flourish, bloom, be themselves, finally. By the end of this first program, I not only knew that I was going to leave the corporate world to set up my own company but also I knew that CIYO would keep an important place in my life. And it does. Ten years later, I am very involved in co-hosting CIYO events in various places in the world and supporting women to connect with their authenticity and their own callings. When women change and evolve, they bring positive change around them, to their families and to the organizations they belong to.

"To live is to choose. But to choose well,
you must know who you are and
what you stand for,

where you want to go and why
you want to get there."

Kofi Annan

Having courage

While reconnecting with my wholeness, my decision was clear. I wanted to keep my energy and my passion around the topic of Diversity & Inclusion. I finally respected my calling, deeply rooted in my heart: I wanted and still want to be a positive force for change, for a better world where people could be themselves, with no pressure to wear masks. People who could respect each other, work together inclusively, be at peace, learn and grow with each other. Encouraging people to look at the positive side of life. Being myself and supporting others to be themselves. It is a journey. It is not easy. And yet, it is a mindset. A willingness to find a place in the world and helping others to find theirs. I suddenly felt the urgency to create my own consulting business to be free and honor myself.

"I learned that courage was not the absence of fear,
but the triumph over it.

The brave man is not he who does not feel afraid,
but he who conquers that fear."

Nelson Mandela

3. Creating Pluribus

Embedding key values

From the moment I founded Pluribus, I wanted to live the mission of Pluribus in my bones. You don't promote diversity and inclusion only from your head. You need to walk the talk. You need to have it from your heart, deep inside. My mission and the mission of Pluribus is to support individuals, teams and organizations to create an environment where everyone feels listened to, valued, respected and included so she or he can fulfill her or his full potential.

> - Diversity: visible and invisible differences and similarities that make us unique
>
> - Inclusion: willingness and capability of valuing and capitalizing on the various diversity facets

When I started to build the Pluribus network, it was important that the new facilitators could equally resonate with this mission and embed these key values. We are not teachers in diversity and inclusion. We want to be role models in diversity and inclusion. It is a life journey as we are continuously learning and challenging ourselves. Humility is certainly one of the qualities promoting diversity and inclusion. We need humility to recognize that working with diverse teams and building inclusion is complex. It does not happen overnight. There is no magical recipe. We need to challenge our mental models consistently, our biases, all the stereotypes and clichés which have influenced us implicitly or explicitly. Humility to see that we are not perfect, the workplace is not perfect, and yet we are good enough. We are good enough to learn about ourselves, our biases and our strengths. So we can do better, so the workplace evolves. All is mainly unconscious as research shows, how this humbles each one of us, as we all have biases, and discriminate somehow. This makes the work we do deeply personal and intimate. A work that invites self-reflection, vulnerability, courage and authenticity. Work that can profoundly shift individuals and organizations.

I believe that the Pluribus network is a true laboratory of diversity and inclusion. With more than 50 people based all over the world, more than 16 spoken languages, men and women from different generations, cultures, backgrounds, religions, we are actually testing, learning, growing together. So as D&I facilitators, we need to truly embed some key values to be congruent: trust, transparency, generosity, respect and inclusion.

Trust in each other on a personal level and trust in our capacities as professionals. Trust also to create together the necessary change for more diversity and inclusion practices. And last but not least, trust that projects will emerge whenever and wherever our input is being asked for.

Transparency in the way we communicate among us, either on personal or professional matters, but also transparency in contact with each other and toward our clients. We intentionally promote transparency in our remuneration process so everyone feels part of the process.

Generosity in the way we communicate and learn from each other. Generosity in sharing responsibly our benefits.

Respect for the uniqueness of each contributor is also fundamental and woven into the deep-felt understanding that each single one of us has an impact to make to the unfolding and positive change the world is asking for.

Inclusion – being seen and listened to for who we are, naturally with no mask. Capitalizing and optimizing what everyone can bring.

"If you want to know someone, do not listen to what he says but look at what he does."

Dalai Lama

Honoring all the different roles

And this translates in various roles we play within the network. These roles are varied, ranging from business developers, key accounts and facilitators to strategic thinkers, program developers, and last but not least, back office and financial supporters. Several of us wear double and triple hats.

All of us are independent and experienced professionals working alone or in collaborations with other organizations as well. We are all "glocal" (global and local) in our mindsets, yet some work mainly in one region, others work globally in various continents and in various languages.

Together we can develop and experience the beauty and the challenges of a new economic model, which is based on individual responsibility for our own and the well-being of the whole organization, be it our own or one of our clients. I do my best to reinforce our community of practice, stand still to look at how this laboratory has an impact on our own lives and see how we can inspire each other even more. Together we can make it happen!

"Don't walk behind me, I may not lead. Don't walk in front of me, I may not follow.

Just walk beside me and be my friend."

Albert Camus

4. Celebrating ten years of adventures and discoveries

Instiling and nourished by passion

Ten years of passion for people. Just thinking about all the D&I projects we have initiated or are currently developing in various continents by working together in various contexts, cultures and organizations makes me truly happy.

I can't relate all the anecdotes based on what happened while traveling around the world from Russia to Israel, from Mexico to Singapore, from Istanbul to Dubai, each time for various projects and with different organizations. I feel fortunate to meet so many wonderful and unique people across the globe.

"What counts in life is not the mere fact that we have lived.

It is what difference we have made to the lives of others

that will determine the significance of the life we lead."

Nelson Mandela

Shifting integral role

My role within Pluribus is evolving. It is more about holding the space, the field of possibility for Pluribus. I am more in practicing the being than in the process of the doing. Being present and available for our clients, for the team. To support, mentor and listen. To create space for "what wants to happen." Being aware of my well-being and my body. Respecting stillness. Being more with my family and my friends. This shift allows me to ground my active role as an inclusive leader and founder in a different way. And this makes me happy!

"Yesterday I was clever so I wanted to change the world.

Today I am wise, so I am changing myself."

Rumi

ISABELLE PUJOL

Isabelle Pujol is Founder and Director of Pluribus, a global consultancy committed to developing individuals, teams and organizations to succeed through diversity and inclusion.

With her cross-cultural team of passionate D&I practitioners, she provides strategic consulting and designs and facilitates conversations with leaders from high-performing global organizations to create truly inclusive performing cultures. Key clients are from various sectors and industries: Sodexo, L'Oréal, Hilti, PMI, Nestlé, Carrefour, Total, bpost, Reed Elsevier, Sanofi and Solvay, with projects across the world.

Before founding Pluribus in November 2006, she was one of the pioneering D&I managers in Europe by creating and implementing the first D&I strategy of the BP group in 1998. BP received the Catalyst Award in March 2006 for recognition of its successful global D&I strategy.

Isabelle is determined to play a positive role in the world. She is passionate about empowering men and women in fulfilling their full potential by finding their unique leadership journey. She therefore strongly promotes effective and respectful communication to help individuals and teams reconnect with their inner voice and authenticity. Ultimately, it is all about feeling listened to, respected and included.

Isabelle is French and lives in Wavre, outside Brussels. She is married to Jean-Marc. They have two children, Raphael and Sarah.

Diversity & Inclusion, a catalyst for the evolution of organizations

by Magda Barceló

Introduction

Diversity & Inclusion (D&I) strategic interventions are known for being good for business. And yet, there is a less obvious but more important reason for engaging in D&I, beyond the mentioned one: this is the fact that diversity and inclusion fosters the evolution of the organization and its individuals.

In this chapter by using the work of Frederic Laloux on the evolution of organizations, we consider the different stages from where organizations operate and explain how D&I enhances the breakthroughs that are found in most evolved organizations, therefore enhancing evolution in organizations from every stage.

What characterizes the Pluribus approach is the grounded beingness of the network of facilitators, and the organization itself, with high levels of self-organization, wholeness while being driven by its evolutionary purpose. From that stance, the different interventions advance specific dimensions of the evolution of organizations, specifically: culture, wholeness and evolutionary purpose.

With this awareness, leaders have the capacity to be more intentional and holding a wider framework as they engage with D&I strategic interventions in the increasing complexity of our times. This will likely result in a stronger impact at all levels: at the evolution of the organization, its individuals and the organization's contribution to the world.

Content

1. Organizational stages of evolution

The evolution of human consciousness as studied and documented by a great number of people – from historians, to anthropologists, philosophers, mystics, psychologists and neuroscientists – has been found to develop in stages. Organizations, as an expression of the same human consciousness, have evolved over time too and correlate with each stage of consciousness. Using Ken Wilber and Jenny Wade's work, Frederic Laloux describes different stages of organizations, all co-existing in the present moment.

Gaining familiarity with the different stages of evolution of organizations is helpful to understand the main drives behind every type of organization, the culture and the type of consciousness of its leaders. But more strongly, I found Laloux's work ground breaking, because from his research with current companies, he has come to discern three breakthroughs that underpin the companies that are most evolved, and wildly successful too. What this implies is that evolution can be orchestrated by creating the right structure, and given the necessary conditions: leadership at the highest developmental stage (Teal) and ownership support.

But before going into organizational stages, what do we mean when we talk about development? In Nick Petrie's words: "There is nothing inherently *better* about being at a higher level of development, just as an adolescent is not *better* than a toddler. However, the fact remains that an adolescent is able to do more, because he or she can think in more sophisticated ways than a toddler. Any level of development is okay; the question is whether that level of development is a good fit for the task at hand." So the question is, what is the task at hand? What is our task at hand as humans? What is the task of our organizations at this particular moment in history? How much complexity is asked of us to handle?

Depending on our stage of development, on the stage of development of the leaders of the company, these questions will be answered differently.

Red organizations

Organizations arising from this stage of consciousness are dominated by an impulsiveness drive. They first appeared in the form of small conquering armies, and today they can be found in the form of street gangs and mafias. The metaphor for these organizations is the "wolf pack," and they function by a continuous use of power in their interpersonal relationships. In these organizations the "alpha wolf" uses the power to maintain his status within the pack. Fear is the glue that rules the organization. They are highly reactive and have a short-term focus. This type of organization thrives in chaotic environments.

The breakthroughs of this type of organization are creating a certain division of labor and implementing the command by authority. They are inherently fragile given the impulsive nature of the people running them, which can render them very unstable: the minute the power is in doubt, someone will attempt to topple it. Other weaknesses of Red organizations are they are poor at planning and strategizing.

Amber organizations

Organizations at this stage are characterized by highly formal roles within a hierarchical pyramid. Top-down command and control is how they operate. In these organizations, stability is valued above all through rigorous processes, and the future is seen as a repetition from the past.

The military and the public school systems are archetypes of Amber organizations. Key breakthroughs of this stage are formal roles, with stable and scalable hierarchies, and processes that enable having a long-term perspective.

One of the limitations of Amber organizations is its hierarchical stratification where moving up the hierarchy can be a non-straightforward thing. The other is the "us" versus "them" where people inside the organizations relate or rather enter into conflict with each other with suspicion; it's the "silos" culture. The same rationale operates with the company and the outside world, where it's seen as "another planet" since social life revolves around corporate life and employment is still considered life-long.

Orange organizations

In the Orange worldview, life can be understood as complex clockwork whose workings can be investigated. The organization is seen as a machine. Modern global corporations are the embodiment of Orange organizations. With them three distinctive breakthroughs were brought: innovation, accountability and meritocracy.

The shadow parts of Orange organizations are growth for the sake of growth, making it environmentally unsustainable with planet depletion as a direct result; success measured just in terms of money and recognition; inequality and corruption.

Green organizations

Within the classic pyramid structure, Green organizations focus on culture and empowerment to achieve extraordinary employee motivation. Some successful examples of this approach are Southwest Airlines and Ben & Jerry's. Their key breakthroughs are employees' empowerment, a values-driven culture and a stakeholder model that takes into account social concerns beyond pure profit. The guiding metaphor for this stage is the organization as a family.

The limitations of Green organizations come from the post-modern world view and stem from its unease with power, rules and hierarchy. When it insists that all perspectives are equal and deserve equal respect in the face of others abusing this stance by putting forward intolerant ideas. Unsuccessful Green approaches are often a result of the failure of consensus in decision making and the rigidity of bottom-up processes. In summary, this paradigm has been great at deconstructing, breaking down old structures, but has proven less effective at formulating practical alternatives.

2. Teal organizations

The metaphor used for Teal organizations is one of a living organism or system. Life in its evolutionary wisdom manages ecosystems ever evolving toward more wholeness, complexity and consciousness. In this case, it is life itself that fuels the organization. Laloux's research encompassing companies from different sizes, cultures and industries, describes three distinctive features they share in common:

- *Wholeness:* In stark contrast to business cultures that only allow for the "professional" self at work, which tends to be highly masculine, rational and cold, Teal organizations, through a set of practices and conducive cultures, invite people they work with to reclaim our inner wholeness and bring all who we are to work.

- *Self-management:* Teal organizations have created systems that transcend and include hierarchy and consensus. These systems allow it to operate efficiently and at a large scale with a system of peer relationships.

- *Evolutionary purpose:* These organizations see themselves as having a life and a sense of direction of their own. Instead of trying to predict the future, members are invited to listen in and understand what the organization wants to become. Connecting the personal purpose with the organizational purpose is sought and encouraged. Profit making becomes a result from following the purpose of the company, instead of the primary goal.

And these three breakthroughs are supported by the key role of *particular cultural traits* as recognized by the leaders of the researched organizations.

Nothing such as a "pure" Teal organization exists, but most of the researched ones are a blend, having innovated in some areas with practices and processes and having more Green or Orange practices in others. And yet, the similarities show that there is consistency and enough correlation to consider these organizations to be part of a different evolutionary stage.

Another thing to consider is that Wholeness, Self-management and Evolutionary purpose reinforce each other. This is because the more self-organized an organization is, the easier it is to be whole and show up as who you really are. The greater freedom to express your vocation or purpose at work, the easier it gets to self-manage in groups that share a common passion connected to the company's purpose. The more accustomed people are to listening to who they are and relating to each other in an authentic and non-ego-based way, the easier it gets to listen collectively to the evolutionary purpose of the organization.

After reading this, you might be asking yourself what's the point of all that if my organization is not at Teal level? Some organizations I have worked with have found it misleading to take Teal as a destination instead of an inspiration, a process worthwhile in itself. By considering the latter, this framework marks the key dimensions necessary to support organizational and personal evolution, and these dimensions are directly connected with the work of diversity and inclusion we do.

3. How it works in practice

Most of the organizations we support are in Orange stage. Some have Green traits. A few have Amber pasts. And others have Teal intentions. They all have in common being formed by people with a desire to evolve along with the organization. Leaders know that there is more, and that they have blind spots they are not seeing, and invite us to support their efforts.

As Parker J. Palmer beautifully proposes, in any training or teaching program, more important than the what (contents), or the how (way of delivering them) is the who. Who are the individuals that facilitate trainings, in our case workshops, experiential learnings, strategic interventions? And for the case being, and since we're considering organizations, what kind of organization is Pluribus?

This is fundamental, because in any intervention there is something that speaks louder than any presentation, any word that's uttered, any email, any question asked or answered. And this is our way of being as facilitators, as humans. We all share a deep passion for this work which has us continually engaged in learning, a commitment to our continuous personal evolution and showing up with high levels of authenticity and vulnerability.

So our beingness gets to the places that need our presence and skills. But how does it get there? How is the organization behind it orchestrating it? How Teal is this organization? Well, the answer that comes is: a great deal. Pluribus does not work with strategic goals or targets. We are an expanding web of freelance consultants who are connected with each other by personal bonds, projects and interests; many of us are friends after having collaborated on many projects. One might find a project and act as project manager for it. This means that after speaking to procurement (part of the minimalist central office) then she will create her ad hoc team for the project. Consulting rates are transparent according to the role. Associates join the projects that appeal to them the most. I recently was offered a collaboration for a company that I didn't feel my values aligned with; I refused the collaboration and my decision was totally respected, having other offers for other projects shortly after. Information and materials are available in a shared drive. And ad hoc mentors take up their roles from their initiative on a volunteer basis, as new projects emerge, to coach facilitators that need support in terms of content, understanding the client or designing an approach.

So having Wholeness and Self-organization, how do we collectively listen to the Evolutionary purpose? While economic sustainability is pursued, it has never been the driving force for Isabelle Pujol, the Founder and CEO. In her words: "Our purpose is to bring the work of D&I into the corporate world. We're fulfilling a need that impacts thousands of people as we support organizations shift their culture toward a more human one. If one day this is no longer needed, it will be great news. All companies will be getting it right. And I have no doubt that we will find other ways to contribute to the world."

The Founder Isabelle Pujol and a core team of facilitators meet once a year in a two-day gathering. This is a time of celebrating successes, sharing our lives and our dreams as we collectively listen to where the organization wants to evolve. And then we come back to our respective lives, staying connected and with stronger bonds that allow for continuous collaboration, learning and inspiration.

4. Enhancing Teal breakthroughs

In concrete terms, this is the *what* we do offer to organizations to advance each of the aforementioned breakthroughs. In each of the dimensions, our approaches combine challenge with support. We fully embrace the place where the organization and its individuals find themselves, and challenge them to move beyond.

A shift in the culture of the organization is a common result of our interventions. Teal leaders recognize the key role of culture in the functioning of the organizations as the invisible water we all swim in. For example, our workshops in Unconscious Bias unearth people's beliefs and mindsets, and how they are linked to their behaviors and the interplay with organizational systems and the organizational culture. The experiential learning nature of the workshop invites high levels of self-discovery, intimacy, and authenticity that when noticing our shared humanity connects people from a level where there is no way back to relate to others as just "colleagues."

In order to support organizations' *Wholeness* our interventions have several components. All of our workshops create safe and open learning environments, through ground rules and facilitated discussions. This is often taken on board by employees participating, especially if they are participating in a Train the Trainer, one of our favorite modalities, where we build internal D&I expertise in the organization that then continues to operate internally once we've left. Authentic relating skills are built through workshops about conversational stances, non-violent communication and conflict resolution. The creation of reflective practices is achieved facilitating with tools like journaling, silence, large group reflections (Open Space, World Café). One-on-one coaching is available to work with leaders at any level, to support their inner wholeness through development. And collective learning is hosted and held through the creation and support of Communities of Practice of individuals that decide to take on this challenge.

In the words of Brian Robertson, the founder of Holacracy, talking about *Evolutionary purpose:* "It's us humans that can tune into the organization's evolutionary purpose; but the key is about separating identity and figuring out 'What is this organization's calling?' not 'What do we want to use this organization to do, as property?' but rather 'What is this life, this living system's creative potential?' That's what we mean by evolutionary purpose: the deepest creative potential to bring something new to life, to contribute something energetically, valuably to the world... It's that creative impulse or potential that we want to tune into, independent of what we want ourselves."

Some of the main tools we use are within what's considered large group processes, like World Café, Open Space, Appreciative Inquiry and Theory U. These are offered to support organizations connect to their evolutionary purpose, by listening to the whole system. And as life itself, once identified, the evolutionary purpose will keep evolving and evolving, and needs to be listened to again and again.

And our work in supporting companies *Self-manage* is yet to start… perhaps you might be interested in starting this line of work?

5. Can you be more intentional as a leader?

Whether you are familiar with D&I work or if you are considering embarking on such, now you have a wider lens through which to consider the scope of these efforts, by asking yourself some of these questions: What is the lens through which I see the world? What is the stage of development of my organization? What would it mean to evolve? What would this make possible at an individual and collective level? What would it make possible for the world?

In practice, if you decide to go for it, be ready to walk the talk, role-modeling all that is learned, as well as to hold space and create and sustain structures for evolution. Both D&I and evolution take practice and commitment. Successful companies take it on as onboarding workshops as they build internal capacities to deliver it, and periodically offer it to existing employees to keep growing, keep deepening in the knowledge of our biases, of the lenses we see the world through, and the impact this has in our work, in the business, and in our lives.

These are exciting times to live in, high complexity, huge challenges, with increasing awareness and loads of support. From my experience, I cannot but encourage you in this ride.

Conclusion

More and more business leaders are engaging in D&I efforts. By considering the big picture of organizational evolution, as a leader you can engage in a deeper way why this matters and support it more intentionally. Yes, it's the right thing to do, yes it's good for the business, and more importantly, it has the potential to support the organization and its individuals to evolve, and as a result equip it to handle higher levels of complexity and positive impact in the world.

Sources:

Laloux, Frederic. *Reinventing Organizations.*
Nelson Parker (2014)

Reinventing Organizations Wiki
http://www.reinventingorganizationswiki.com/
(2016)

Palmer, Parker J. *The Courage to Teach: Exploring the Inner Landscape of a Teacher's Life* (2007)

MAGDA BARCELÓ

Magda Barceló is a certified Integral Coach, organizational consultant and facilitator.

Part of the Pluribus team since 2010 as a Senior Associate, her passion is to support individuals and organizations in realizing their highest potential, through coaching, training and Teal (Integral) organizational practices.

Fluent in five languages, she holds a degree in Business Administration and Masters in Gender and Social Policy from the London School of Economics.

She works internationally and has her home base in Spain where she lives with her family.

She finds great joy in hiking, practicing yoga, writing and painting.

Heart, head and hands

by Cécile Pernette Masson

*"Which is the best government? That which
teaches us to govern ourselves."*

Goethe

Introduction

This chapter explores the relationship between the attitude we
have as individual Diversity & Inclusion professionals and our own
embodied leadership. I will do this by looking at our inner diversity
of intelligences (heart, head and hands), how they relate to our
organs, and the possibilities these offer to be in best alignment with
our own inclusive leadership values. One basic assumption is that
as a human being, we are ourselves a system interacting with other
systems.

The reason why I am personally interested in this field has grown
from the many essential conversations I have had in various settings
with men and women, and from observing their body language.
What intrigued me was that it did not seem that essentially different,
whether the conversation was held in French, German or English.
It was as if their unconscious movements told something about
the various intelligences present in their body. Each intelligence, or
brain as we will see later, expresses itself in another fashion, has a
different speed, and processes the world around in a different way.
They have clearly different prime functions and underlying core
competencies.

Another reason why this subject interests me is that in Switzerland,
where I grew up, the pedagogy of Johan Heinrich Pestalozzi
(1746-1827) has much shaped the education system. His motto
was "Learning by head, hand and heart" which was certainly
revolutionary for his time. His thoughts in many ways influenced
the rich philosophical work of R. Steiner and the work of Carl Jung
who both worked in Zurich and Basel and who later exchanged on

the subject. That was at the end of the 19th century and the Asian philosophies, religions and wisdom were to inspire more and more the work of Western scholars. Their writing has greatly influenced in turn the pioneering work of many change agents worldwide. In many ancient wisdom traditions such as Shamanism, Buddhism, the Jewish Kabbalah, and early Christianity, the three levels of intelligences are well known. At its best, this approach allows the senses to be developed and gives access to a less formative linear experience of the world. It acknowledges for instance what many artists learn to trust: hands have an own "knowing."

All wisdom traditions confirm that our body is a fine organism that treats information in the most delicate manner. It is in constant connection with the outer world that resonates in a more or less agreeable manner with our own. Just think of a full packed subway train. To protect your inner self, you shut down automatically. This automatic response is the job of the Autonomic Nervous System (ANS) that also guides our cardiovascular, respiratory and digestive functions on which we have no or minimal control. This automatic controller is divided into two branches called sympathetic and parasympathetic. The importance of the ANS is that they are greatly connected to the two hemispheres of the head brain: the cardiac brain (heart) and the enteric brain (gut). A good balance between the two sides of the ANS that work in opposite ways is therefore of great importance.

In our communication, in whatever language, this intrinsic knowledge is also reflected. "I cannot stop thinking," accompanied by fingers turning high-speed around the ears, or "I should have followed my heart," making a wide move with both hands from the chest, we recognize that:

"The heart has reasons, the reason does not know." - Pascale

The complex challenges that organizations and leaders face in today's global, visibly and palpably interconnected economy does ask for a new type of generative, adaptive and wise leadership that includes our diversity of brains. It invites change agents and leaders to personally embark on a journey toward wholeness that includes our various intelligences by listening to our gut feeling, being true to our heart and embracing the challenges ahead creatively.

This chapter will lift the veil about the possibilities naturally available to us when conscious of our various intelligences, our ways to deal with the information we receive and how we can transform them in the most effective manner. The more we are conscious that what lives in us systemically also lives in the wider system, the more we progress on our journey of embodied leadership. We then might realize that we have the capacity to actively co-create spaces, business opportunities and living organizational structures that celebrate diversity and embrace the otherness full-heartedly, reflecting in our human interactions the incredible bio-diversity that makes our planet earth a charm in the universe.

The individual qualities of our various intelligences

Heart *intelligence*

> *"Educating the mind without educating the heart is no education at all."*
>
> **Aristotle**

The heart as an organ is the center of our energy field with which we are in dialogue with our environment. It is our heart that processes emotions such as anger, grief, hatred, joy or happiness. It is our heart that guides our values regarding what is important to us, giving structure to our priorities. It is the organ from which our dreams, our desires, our passion surge. From there, the nature of any relationship will take shape whether it is in love, hate, indifference, care or compassion.

The energy of the heart has an incredible reach and is very fast in getting information, much faster than our head. When we meet a person for the first time we may sense sympathy, indifference or dislike before we have even spoken.

Let me give you an example: I was aged eight and for the very first time taking the tram on my own. My parents did not yet have a TV at the time and my knowledge of the world was the one of a middle-class girl grown up in a protected neighborhood. I was dangerously innocent. I remember standing at the tram stop gazing into the far distance where some 300m from me a man was advancing toward the stop. Instinctively I knew that he meant trouble. Something in me told me that I should be on my guard. I had never experienced anything like that before and froze on the spot. And indeed he did come toward me, not taking a no for a no when I refused to join him on a walk in the forest. When he eventually touched me to take me by the arm, I unfroze and ran back home in utter shock.

Looking back at it now, what still surprises me is the distance at which I had already sensed the depraved intentions of this individual. An open heart does not know boundaries and that can give precious information when listened to even though our rational voice may say, "Do not be so difficult," or "He must have just been joking." It may be called the voice of intuition.

When the parasympathetic and sympathetic nervous systems are well balanced, we experience the best of the heart's strength and qualities, qualities such as joy, love, gratitude and compassion. When the two sides are not well balanced, we may experience despair or feel manic instead of joy, apathy and vengefulness instead of compassion, indifference or hate instead of love. It is vital to appreciate and acknowledge when we do not feel quite at ease in a situation as this might give us important clues about ourselves but also about the place we are in.

The heart is the very core from which the generative, inclusive leadership attitude is nestled that offers generously the space to others to express their uniqueness, appreciating their difference in thinking, functioning or physical make-up.

The essential question addressed from the heart is:

How should I **be** to effectively address challenges in my surroundings?

Head *intelligence*

> *"As long as she thinks of a man, nobody objects to a woman thinking."*
>
> Virginia Woolf, *Orlando*

From the three intelligences described in this chapter, the head intelligence is probably the one best known. In the Western world and culture, we have been trained to use our head brains to learn facts and acquire intellectual analytical skills. It is the one intelligence that seems to dominate our world and has been skilfully trained for high performance.

The head brain has, as prime function, the cognitive perception that does recognize patterns. With our head we make meaning by thinking, by perceiving the reality in a certain way, also having the capacity of discernment. The discernment invites to reasoning, to structural argumentations, abstraction, analysis, synthesis and also metacognition that allows us to observe and be aware of our very own thinking patterns. From all that thinking and analyzing we actually make meaning and express that through semantic processing. We will have encoded the meaning of "Once upon a time, there was…" as being the beginning of a fairy tale, that invites all English speakers to listen with another ear than when hearing the beginning of a speech that starts "Ladies and Gentlemen…" The head intelligence equally gives us access to understanding the language of metaphor that brings in yet another level of cognition especially appreciated by poets and pioneering minds.

In the context of D&I, it is that intelligence that might be used to discern the patterns of prejudice, of systematic discrimination or unconstructive ways of communicating. Since the late 19th century and two consecutive world wars, women have been active more visibly in the workforce. However, the mindset in which they widely operate has not adapted to this fact.

Some women thankfully have taken their own thoughts and cognitive capacities seriously enough. The pioneer's social background has privileged them to be educated as a man but they went beyond, not denying their own womanhood. In the 19th and 20th centuries, this has helped many gender-related changes to be implemented in the wider social field. The British Museum that in the 1920s refused my grandmother as an employee because she was a woman, now since many decades has women staff who not only do excellent historical research but also work in the field of conservation and restoration. However, just to illustrate how much work still needs to be done, it was only in 2014 that some European member states signed the Istanbul Convention making it a human right for women and children (of both sexes) to be free of domestic violence and abuse, be that sexual, physical, or mental.

Having said that, the head's intelligence does not only discern patterns but also creates learning methodologies to create a much-desired inclusive work environment. It is that intelligence that when lived well allows us to be fully present, that allows us to have an integrated view upon the world and ourselves. When at its best it is the opening to curiosity instead of fixation and opens the very channel to creativity.

The essential question from the head is:

What is worth **knowing** so that I can serve my surroundings well? (What questions are worth asking, which theoretical frameworks, skills.)

Hands (gut) *intelligence*

"Never ignore a gut feeling,
but never believe that it's enough."

Robert Heller

The third intelligence, the enteric or gut intelligence, is metaphorically linked to our hands. We all know expressions like "I had a gut feeling about this…"

The enteric intelligence that we experience as a drive in our guts and express through our hands invites us to be in the doing, to act. It is the intelligence that invites us to bring forward practical solutions. Sometimes a gut reaction can save our lives, like when the house is on fire; sometimes it just indicates a malaise. But there again it is useful to be able to differentiate the messages.

The gut "brain" is the first neurological system that develops in the human embryo. It has been the intelligence that during our human evolution has protected us on the most basic survival level. Self-preservation and mobilization to action is its prime function. At its best it is the one that indicates when we are hungry, that gives us courage: *"It really took a lot of guts to say that,"* or that gives us a state of well-being and relaxation: *"I have a healthy appetite for life."* When the parasympathetic and sympathetic side are not well balanced, however, hunger might become lust or disgust; courage might become withdrawal or fight; calmness might become anxiety or depression. It is that guttural intelligence that made me freeze and unfreeze when harassed by the man at the tram stop.

In that area of our body much emotional information is stored. Passed traumas or emotional blockages are "saved" there and when not released can create serious health problems. It is surprising maybe, but that is where our core identity is nestled.

Realization processes that D&I might be useful often start from the enteric intelligence. Let me give you an example. A manager in a big organization realizes that things need to evolve. She has a vague idea, knows that it has something to do with fixed assumptions and would like to see a rapid transformation realized also from a strategic point of view for business development. She has had enough of certain unconstructive behavior, especially gender related. "She has had enough" is a signal of satiety and she is "hungry" for change. She takes her courage by the hand, realizes that if she does not act courageously to bring forth that change nothing will ever alter. She takes the initiative, reaches out to colleagues and experts and things start moving in the direction of the desired adjustments. The spark comes from the realization of "enough" which indicates that her gut is full of the prejudices, the unconscious biases from both genders and of out-served cultural mindsets.

The essential question from the hands or enteric intelligence is:

What should/can I **do** to collaboratively lead my surroundings to the desired change?

How to constructively use the awareness of these three intelligences that are active in and through me?

"It takes something more than intelligence to act intelligently."

Fyodor Dostoyevsky, *Crime and Punishment*

The governing norm of intelligence active in the global economy and research at this moment in time is arguably the cognitive intelligence that has been trained intensively accepting the dual separation of body and mind. However, if we look at society worldwide, other intelligences keep challenging this norm because of cultural values, ancient wisdoms and simply because of our human make-up. More and more people, change agents and leaders realize at some point that organizations, and any form of human interaction, is much more than just a theoretical framework and move away from the mechanical structuring of processes to a more flexible and organic organizational shape. They leave the restrictive awareness of "head on legs" and adopt a more holistic perception of the world. This conscious integration of the various intelligences can bring forth a more inclusive attitude. To work on this, some have included mindfulness practices in their daily routine, use storytelling to train empathetic listening or develop a team spirit. Systems thinking and systemic work shows that much information is unconsciously active in the field that could be useful when made conscious. Much research shows that meditating and mindfulness practices have a hugely positive impact because it develops the awareness of one's own responsibility and place within a greater field. It helps to focus when needed and can be a great tool to manage stressful situations.

However, to really create a generative inclusive environment where diversity is valued and not rejected, more seems to be necessary.

The scientists Grant Soosalu and Marvin Oka show that the balancing of the ANS through conscious breathing that lasts as long in the inhaling as exhaling phase, that is contrary to most breathing habits, helps to release tensions. They also have shown with extensive research that all ancient wisdom traditions have acknowledged and integrated these three brains that we experience energetically in our bodies. By looking at the various ways the wisdom traditions have done it and overlapping it to data from the latest neuroscientific research, they realized that the awareness of these different intelligences is one thing but to be using them effectively to bring forth the desired change for personal, organizational or community improvement is another.

In the West, as I wrote earlier on, the cognitive intelligence dominates. By allowing the cognitive intelligence to take a step back, like many do when running or gardening, we can experience a state of an "empty head" that is most pleasant as the ANS are in balance. Often solutions appear that previously were not feasible. Allowing other intelligences to work with the head, such as the hands, we then give the cognitive intelligence its appropriate place.

The importance is to align our internal communication between the three Hs well and in certain sequence to allow all three to express their highest potential from where true wisdom can surge. According to Soosalu and Oka, the highest potential for the heart (cardiac brain) is compassion, for the head (cephalic brain) it is creativity and for the gut or hands (enteric brain) it is courage. Allowing our heart to give us information, listening to our gut and checking it with our head gives us a new dynamic.

They figured out that the most effective "roadmap" to any change and healthy decision making is heart-head-heart-gut (hands)-heart, acknowledging that change-making information travels upward and is aligned to the heart rather than the head.

Conclusion

*"Where the spirit does not work with the hand, there
is no art."*

Leonardo da Vinci

In the context of change, decision making and obviously also
D&I, respecting that sequence in the strategic planning, the design
of programs, and most evidently in the embodiment of the key
change agents and leaders is a great source of wisdom. However,
none of us are all the time in perfect alignment from within as we
are continuously interacting with our surroundings like a dancer.
Nonetheless, having a heightened awareness of the signals we
receive through and from our own body can help us on the way.
We can embrace a lifelong dialogue with ourselves to assimilate all
of our being in any interaction with others. The self-awareness and
self-facilitation for integrating heartfelt values with head-centered
intellect and gut-based instincts is key to being a generative and
adaptive change maker or leader.

Yet the form is not so much a question of a new (leadership) style
anymore. The form itself is found through the authentic, tangible
and conscious embodiment with which we impact others. To
express the trinity of the Heart, the Head and the Hands wisely is
an art, and D&I as a discipline is one of its many forms.

Main sources

C. Jung: various books

Ken Wilber: various

Dalai Lamas http://www.dalailamafellows.org/program/heart-head-and-hands

Grant Soosalu & Marvin Oka: *mBraining*

The Bible

The Women's Leadership Program, Coming Into Your Own and its Global Community

Rudolf Steiner: various books

Gregg Braden: various

University of Life

Johan Heindrich Pestalozzi 1746-1827: I was lucky to still benefit in the 1960s and 1970s from his motto: Education through head, heart and hand

CÉCILE PERNETTE MASSON

Cécile Pernette is a coach, leadership retreat facilitator, multilingual trainer and systemic thinking partner. Her focus is on leadership development, diversity and inclusion, and holding essential conversations that address personal, collective and global challenges.

The purpose of her work is to co-create meaningful results that empower individuals, teams and organizations.

As a social entrepreneur for more than 15 years, she is particularly passionate about the personal journey of leaders toward wholeness and the role and power of feminine leadership to support sociocultural transformations related to mindsets and economic impact.

Her business experience bridges a variety of sectors in several European countries – the arts, global energy, NGOs, regional government and education.

Cécile Pernette is Swiss and is fully proficient in Dutch, English, French, Italian and has a complete understanding of German. She believes in the effectiveness of collective and cohesive wisdom that is based on fundamental trust, co-responsibility and wholeness. Her passion for the human spirit pervades her work; nature and the arts are her main sources of inspiration.

Cécile Pernette joined the Pluribus network as a Senior Associate in 2012 and is involved in various D&I projects in different regions.

Gender balance:
it starts from within

by Burcu Yalman

I am the big sister in a Turkish family with two children. My brother is five years younger than me. I have always heard from my parents that we were born with mixed sexualities; I was too assertive, self-confident, extravert, energetic, perseverant, ambitious, independent, analytical for a girl and my brother was too emotional, introvert, adaptive, compassionate, empathetic, calm for a boy. "You should have been a boy," was not only the words of my parents, but also many of my teachers, my friends, even my boyfriends, later on my colleagues and also the astrologists I went to. What was wrong with me?

Yes, I was a tomboy. Leaving home at the age of 11 to get a good education, I had to be a strong, independent, self-sufficient teenager, solving her problems by herself and not causing any burden on anybody. Also, to minimize any potential risk (probably it looked like a risk to me at that age), the best way was to hide my teenage girl beauty (a brunette with long hair and big green eyes was definitely "different" and "catchy") and emphasize my great friendship capacity among boys. I was not a "typical" girl – whatever it meant to me at that time – and was so proud of it.

This continued during high school and university years. Most of my friends were male; I felt more comfortable and got along better with them rather than the females of my age. When I started having intimate relationships, I began discovering my feminine side, which was still a secret to many. I was still perceived as a powerful young woman, while surprisingly my definition was rather a powerful young person. My woman identity did not fully occur to me until I became a mother. Still, during that time I was once warned by my husband that the family did not need two fathers!

Always encouraged and acknowledged by my parents to be independent and strong, earning my own living and standing on my feet had become my primary target in life; not depending on a husband's income, title or reputation to find my place in the world was like the ultimate purpose. Gaining my father's pride in this regard had always been the biggest award. I was a successful student, got my education from top notch local and foreign institutions, I was a successful professional, starting my career at the World Bank in Washington DC at the age of 25, and continuing in Turkish and international finance institutions at various managerial levels. I was a successful entrepreneur leading my corporate advisory firm at the age of 36 working primarily with foreign private equity funds.

Throughout those years, I was exposed to many incidents which I did not realize at that time would be great diversity and inclusion stories that I would share years after in my D&I workshops as unique, striking cases with lessons learned. Let me share one of such stories here with you.

At the age of 28, working in the corporate finance team of a financial institution, I was the only woman in the team. Single with no kids, life was almost fully spent in the office, days and nights, weekdays, weekends, from one project to another. As if we were living a tribal life, or in a boys' school, with the exception of myself. One night, again working in the office in front of my computer, probably doing valuations, the gang (five young men, my colleagues and also good friends) came over to my desk and said: "We took a decision concerning you: from now onwards, we will call you Osman" (a typical Turkish male name, which comes from Ottoman). I asked why. "Well, this way, we will feel more comfortable and we will be able to tell dirty jokes, talk about manly matters more easily." At first I felt very disappointed: despite my nature, they still perceived me as a typical woman, not one of them. Then, I felt happy: they still wanted to include me in their gang, and not feel that I was a woman. I did not realize that this could only happen at the cost of my name. And, literally, they called me Osman from there on, and I quickly adapted to my new name, in fact was very happy with it, as it underlined that I was not a "typical woman!" What a shame.

Today, I am working with corporations on many diversity aspects, including gender balance. However, to be able to do what I do now,

I had to start the work with myself. How was the gender balance within me? Was I inclusive to my feminine side? What were my unconscious biases against women, femininity? How could I accept and embrace my wholeness, including my female nature, my womanhood? What were the virtues that I would have gained if I were more inclusive to my feminine side? This inner work has taken many years, and is still going on. On the way, I have realized that the best teachers in a subject are those who learn about that subject through their life experiences, and from the hard way. Also, what I have realized is that the best way to master something is to teach it. So, my path led me to a place where I found myself working with women, assisting them to access their wholeness, embrace their feminine nature and attain gender balance within themselves. What I see now in my society is that I was not alone, my case was not unique; many successful, independent, assertive, career-oriented women suffer from not being inclusive to their feminine side. Some realize that they suffer, some do not.

While this is the case on a personal level, how can we attain gender balance in organizations by just balancing the gender ratio in the number of employees? Having 50% men and 50% men-like women – does this solve the issue of gender balance? Most companies are not even aware that there is such an issue, by looking only at the surface and not realizing the ongoing assimilation.

"We treat all our male and female employees equally. Gender is not an issue for us." This is the answer I get from most of the companies. This is the very first level of awareness in diversity and inclusion: **Denial** because *"I don't know what I don't know."* The reality is men and women are different: they are different in nature, different in needs, different in culture. Therefore, treating them as if they are equal does not create fairness in the work environment. On the contrary, it reinforces the secret myth that as we treat women and men alike, they should behave alike.

"Yes, we are very much aware of the importance of women in the workforce and have identified women as our key diversity target. However, we have received reaction from both men and women. So, emphasizing on differences is risky in a work environment." This is how companies in the second level of awareness will respond: **Defensiveness** which is *"I know what I did not know and tried, but emphasis on differences is threatening."* In such cases, usually the trial may include trainings specifically designed for and offered to women, such as feminine leadership development, awareness raising activities across all employees about woman in the workforce, equal opportunity etc., or seminars, guest speakers, even some sort of social responsibility projects supporting increased levels of participation by women in business life and economy. It is a pleasure to see that at least one dimension of diversity – gender – has become the area of focus, but only one part of it – woman – has been able to enter into the spotlight. When companies miss the whole diversity topic and focus on only one part of it, such as woman instead of gender, then this focus may not only attract negative reaction from the other part (e.g. men) but may also create disturbance within the part of focus, namely women: *"Why are we put under the spotlights? Are we not as strong, as good, as competent as our male counterparts, as managers or leaders?"*

"Gender balance is a key diversity focus in our company. We have already taken concrete steps toward equal man-woman ratio in all levels of employees from specialists to top management, and in all functions. We target at least 60-40 man-woman ratio." This answer indicates the third level of awareness in diversity and inclusion: **Acceptance** that is *"I accept the differences in gender, see the inequality and am willing to do something about it."* According to this approach, the easiest and quickest remedy to quantitative inequality prevailing in companies seems to be to introduce man-woman ratio requirements in the workforce and take recruitment and promotion as the main areas for action. Decision makers are expected to prioritize women over men in their decision to recruit and promote with the focus to fulfill a quota system. This is called positive discrimination, which means an action that is aimed at

getting rid of past or actual discriminations undergone by a group of people, by temporarily giving them preferential treatment. Although the intention is positive, which is to create equality, the impact on employees may not be that positive. Nevertheless, it is still a kind of discrimination and therefore usually creates controversial reactions and might even be illegal in some countries. Some companies have chosen to pursue this approach in obliging recruiting professionals to maintain a 50-50 man-woman ratio in identifying candidates for vacancies. In other words, recruiters are required to find the same number of candidates from both genders to secure giving equal opportunity to both men and women in hiring. The ratio in the existing workforce is not the main focus nor the priority.

In this regard, another way to tackle possible resistance is to introduce the ratio in workforce not specifically for women or men but for both genders. In such cases, for instance, the targeted ratio is set as 60-40% for any gender. This approach would put women into the priority in functions/levels where men's ratio exceeds 60%, or similarly men in functions/levels where women's ratio exceeds 60%. Both strategies explained above are effective ways to tackle and at least minimize the possible resistance and reaction which may come from the employees due to the negative perception of positive discrimination and strongly focus on positive action.

"Gender balance is our key priority. But what matters for us is not only the quantitative gender balance and therefore not meeting some ratio targets, but more to create a qualitative gender balance where both masculine and feminine cultures and leadership traits, natures and needs are welcome and even so are encouraged." This answer indicates the fourth and final level of diversity and inclusion awareness in corporations which is **Internalization**: *"I value both visible and invisible differences in gender and I know a holistic approach to balance, that means both quantitative and qualitative, can only be achieved if I respect and nurture both invisible and visible differences."* This type of response is in fact rare to encounter.

If we use the iceberg metaphor to explain this, I would call *advanced* diversity and inclusion approach companies do not perceive the issue only as the tip of the iceberg on the surface. They are aware that there is a whole much bigger part lying underneath the surface, which points out all the gender cultural differences between men and women.

When I use gender culture, I usually get puzzled facial expressions, comments and inquiries. Culture is usually associated with the concept of nation, ethnicity or sometimes religion. Talking about culture in the context of gender is not common. However, similar to nation, ethnicity, and/or religion, gender dimension of diversity involves differences in culture as well.

This culture is affected from the moment we were born, not only by geography, country, culture, era, but mostly by the family in which we were born. There are some common patterns and stereotypes and also some unique cases. Realizing those are the first steps toward internalizing what is in our nature first and then accepting these as virtues in our outer world. Therefore, companies focusing on gender balance should first start with raising individual awareness of their employees about their relationship with their own gender as well as the opposite gender, meaning their conscious and unconscious biases; what they include and exclude in themselves; how they perceive both genders and the relationship between gender and a successful career or being a strong leader.

All successful transformations start with self-awareness. Here is an inquiry for you to reflect on: What parts of yourself do you judge, suppress or exclude? Which gender culture do you think they relate to?

BURCU YALMAN

Burcu is Pluribus Turkey Country Manager since 2011. She has worked in various leadership and coaching programs, offered various Diversity & Inclusion workshops, seminars, Train the Trainer programs to multinationals in Turkey and CEE & MEA regions, e.g. Cargill, L'Oréal, Siemens, Colgate, Unilever, 3M, Nestlé Waters and Philip Morris.

Burcu brings 20 years' of work experience gained in different managerial roles at various international and local organizations and as an entrepreneur. She started her career in 1996 at the World Bank and throughout her 13 years in advisory and corporate finance worked in diverse settings such as the U.S., Turkey, Jordan, Egypt, Pakistan, Sri Lanka, Romania, Bulgaria and Hungary.

Since 2009, Burcu works as a coach and facilitator on leadership and D&I focusing on development of people and enhancement of dialogue in the work environment. She is an ICF certified professional coach, ORSC trained team coach and faculty leader in Adler International, training professional coaches. Also, she is one of the global faculty leaders of Coming Into Your Own, an inner leadership program for women offered for 20 years around the world.

Burcu holds a BA in Business Administration from Boğaziçi University and an MBA from George Washington. She speaks English and French.

Curiosity, culture and inclusion

by Kingsley Weber

"How can you adapt your individual wiring to create and build an inclusive environment?"

Introduction

"One of the challenges of diversity lies in the fact that it cuts into the core personal beliefs and values that one grew up with. The focus of diversity initiatives is to help employees understand why diversity is important and how they can embrace individual differences in their workplace. But the culture change takes time. The company is constantly put under pressure to make short-term business results while creating a culture that respects inclusion and diversity." – CEO Pharma company operating in Asia.

So how do an organization's leaders develop an inclusive culture that honors and respects the differences that each of us bring to the workplace? It is not just about gender and ethnicity; it's much more complex than that.

From my experience of working with Pluribus and our customers operating in a wide range of industries, I strongly believe there are some common denominators. These denominators boil down to how we behave as leaders and how sincere our intent is to be inclusive. The two attributes that shine through again and again with the leaders who I would call truly inclusive are curiosity and self-awareness. The problem is these attributes cannot be taught on a training event; they have to be developed primarily on the job.

"Curiosity killed the cat" is a typical British expression which means inquisitiveness can lead you into dangerous situations. I came across this expression many times when growing up and asking lots of questions of adult family members and their friends. Many times, the common response was simply "don't ask just do it!" Then we arrive as young adults to the world of work, either as a new team member or even as a leader. When I joined corporate life in the 70s, the common responses to my questions were similar to my childhood; along the lines of "but Kingsley that's the way we always do it."

Yet, in today's fast-paced world, without very strong communication skills, innate curiosity and asking open questions, how are you going to deal with the complexity that faces us each day as leaders working globally, within and across cultures? Globally does not necessarily mean that you are traveling to different continents. The diversity of cultures and behaviors impacts us every day as we communicate across boundaries within and outside our companies through email, Skype, phone and in person.

I am fortunate and blessed to have worked and lived in more than 30 countries throughout my career in corporate life and consulting. I have met and worked with some exceptional leaders as well as some poor ones; they were usually in the wrong place at the wrong time, but while they existed in their roles they caused some pain and delay to delivering expected results. However, many did not learn why until some time later when a peer or a boss or a coach gave them direct and unfiltered feedback. Over the next few pages I want to share with you some of the insights I have learned, some the hard way, and offer you food for thought and action as you travel through your own journey of creating and building an inclusive environment, where everyone feels they can contribute and thrive.

The chapter will include thoughts and insights that I have found useful in my own journey of understanding diversity and inclusion, some you may have already learned and/or used yourself. I will share examples to illustrate where leaders have got it wrong or right. I want to encourage you to think about what it takes to build an inclusive environment. I will also share with you some of my observations from my own personal experiences through the maze and complexities of cultures.

There are many definitions of culture in the academic and business fields; my own interpretation of culture is an amalgam of those I have come across and prefer:

"Culture is how we do things around here, which is a system of behaviors that help us act in an accepted and familiar way."

You can see how this expression of culture can impact the way we understand the world around us. Our roots shape our world and this heritage handed down through generations leads to preconceptions of the world around us, which plays out in the business environment at work.

The lessons taught to us as we were being brought up from parents, school, local society, religion and the media become our unconscious beliefs and values. These are the lenses we use to judge others and ourselves.

Layers of difference

Culture is not limited to continents or countries but includes layers of difference we meet every day. These layers of difference illustrate the need for a tool that would help people's social identities:

Core element: personality

Primary dimensions: age, ethnicity, sexual orientation, physical ability, thinking style and gender

Personal/Cultural dimensions: marital status, parental status, work background, personal habits, social status, nationality, language/accent, military experiences, appearance, hobbies/recreation, educational background, religious beliefs, work style, income, geographic location

Organizational dimensions: level/seniority, function, management status, division/department/unit/group, title, work content/field, work location, union affiliation

The challenge for us as leaders is to be genuinely curious about our differences and learn how to embrace and engage this diversity to create success at work.

Reflection exercise

Please study the Layers of Difference model and tick how many of those 30 dimensions you have met working with others in your current role.

Then reflect on yourself and tick four differences that define you. That is to say, if I asked you to describe what makes you tick, which four would you choose while being aware of the layers they sit within:

Biological, Personal/Cultural or Organizational.

I use this Layers of Difference tool during workshops with leaders to illustrate how differences are many and complex, and how we meet nearly all these dimensions of diversity regularly in the workplace. In fact, most people tick more than 27 of the 30 dimensions.

Each one of us becomes a culture in our own way because we are influenced and shaped by the different layers we meet, which needs to be understood and respected. When I asked you to choose the four differences that define you, where did they sit? The majority of leaders I work with have three of their dimensions in the first two layers – Biological and Personal/Cultural – and one in the Organizational layer. Rarely do I find leaders marking two dimensions in the outer layer.

So here is a thought provoker for leaders like you wanting to make an impact. In the work environment we tend to look at people and the roles they play, but their motivation, i.e. what makes them tick, comes from how they define themselves. So how would you connect with them?

These two inner layers are the most private and not easy to broach in the work context, yet if we do not find a way of getting to know the person, how do we know if we are getting the best from them? Not everyone brings their whole self to work; some leave their innermost layers at the door.

"Be like me" and the 7/11 rule

I mentioned wiring at the beginning of the chapter. This refers to the way our values, beliefs and environment shape the way our brains are wired and how this can have an impact on the way we deal with other cultures or people not the same as us. This unconscious bias is investigated in the fast-growing field of cultural neuroscience, which is finding that culture influences brain development, and perhaps vice versa. As much as I would love to, this chapter doesn't have enough pages to travel down this path, but for you as a professional or maybe someone who is interested in cultural differences and how they are formed, it is worth thinking about how we could change our own wiring by seeing the world from different perspectives. The best way to do this is to immerse yourself in another culture, but many of us do not have the luxury of this opportunity as our lives or jobs may be too transient.

Your brain and therefore your wiring plays a massive role in the way you connect with others. Imagine you meet a businessperson for the first time; it could be your new boss, a recent addition to your team, or a potential key account client. The moment that stranger sees you, his or her brain makes a thousand computations: Are you someone to approach or to avoid? Are you friend or foe? Do you have status and authority? Are you trustworthy, approachable, competent, likeable and confident?

And all these computations are made at lightning speed – making major decisions and judgments about each other in the first seven seconds of meeting. In selling and persuasion we sometimes call this the 7/11 rule: where we make at least 11 judgments of another in the first seven seconds. Neuroscientists have found that in less than a blink of an eye we identify gender in 50 milliseconds and racial background in only twice that time. Other observations such as age, disability, space and eyes follow very quickly afterwards.

In business interactions, especially cross-culturally, these first impressions are crucial. You can't stop people from making snap decisions about you, or you them – the human brain is hardwired in this way as a prehistoric survival mechanism, with the limbic brain kicking in.

First impressions are more heavily influenced by nonverbal cues than verbal cues. In fact, studies have found that nonverbal cues have over four times the impact on the impression you make than anything you say. The positive side of this dilemma is that you can learn some tools to help you manage the first few crucial seconds. But if you get this wrong, these subtle and sometimes not so subtle inequities mean that you are judged and placed in a box at the unconscious level and you may never leave this box however hard you try.

So how do you as a culturally connected leader initially build rapport with others not like you? I have watched and studied the behaviors of leaders who make an effort and an impact with others "not like me."

Here are seven nonverbal ways to make a positive first impression:

1. Be aware of and adjust your attitude. People pick up your attitude instantly. Before you turn to greet someone or a group, think about the situation and make a conscious choice about the attitude you want to embody.

2. Be grounded. Confidence is portrayed by occupying the space but in a non-aggressive manner.

3. Smile. A smile, the easiest and most basic tool at our disposal is an invitation, a sign of welcome. It says: "I'm friendly and approachable."

4. Make eye contact. Looking at someone's eyes transmits energy and indicates interest and openness. (To improve your eye contact, make a practice of noticing the eye color of everyone you meet.)

5. Raise your eyebrows. Open your eyes slightly more than normal to simulate the "eyebrow flash" that is the universal signal of recognition and acknowledgement.

6. Greet according to the cultural norm. In some cultures this may mean touching your own heart or shaking hands. This is the quickest way to establish rapport. It's also the most effective. Research shows it takes an average of three hours of continuous interaction to develop the same level of rapport that you can get with a single handshake or culturally sensitive welcome.

7. Lean in slightly. Leaning forward shows you're curious, engaged and interested. But be respectful of the other person's space.

These rules are not rocket science but try them and you might be intrigued and even surprised by the reactions you get.

Frank, a well-respected and high-flying Dutch marketing manager with a global pharmaceutical company had been promoted to lead a business unit in Malaysia. His style of leadership was a shock to the local company; within a year, 70% of his team had resigned or been headhunted. His challenging, and what he thought humorous and sarcastic banter, alienated him from others and created a fear culture. He would reprimand his business managers in public and would interrupt them if he felt their ideas were not up to his standards. As a last resort, I was asked by his regional director to coach Frank before the company decided what to do.

What became clear in our first meeting was that even though Frank had read the books on Malaysian culture and how to do business in Asia, and he had even talked to several peers before starting his job, he was not self-aware and had little sense of the impact he was having on others. He couldn't get his head around the fact that in the Asian culture we do not challenge our bosses in public, and idea generation is a team dynamic and not individualistic. Frank didn't get to know his staff as individuals but saw them as a means to his own end.

The lack of self (and other) awareness and his incredulity when being given feedback about his behavior led the organization to send him back to Europe and to try and repair the loss of confidence within the team.

The investment in Frank has cost the company a great deal both financially and in terms of their credibility in the Asian market.

We share a common space at work but our perceptions are very different.

Is it possible that someone who is 1.88 meters (6 feet 2 inches) will have a different experience at work than someone who is 1.65 meters (5 feet 4 inches)? Is it possible that someone in a wheelchair will have different experience at work than someone who is able bodied? Is it also possible that a Gen Xer will have a different experience from a Gen Yer in the workplace?

Is it possible that a person whose first language is not the mother tongue of the organization will have a different experience from their peers?

The answer of course is yes, but when you ask how and why then some of our unconscious cultural wiring comes into play.

For example, in the U.S. about 14.5% of all men are 1.83 meters (6 feet) or over. Among CEOs of Fortune 500 companies, that number is 58%. Even more strikingly, in the general American population, only 3.9 % of adult men are 1.88 meters (6 feet 2 inches) or taller (source: Malcolm Gladwell, Blink).

I have yet to see research that correlates height with leadership, but in the West especially we meet a tall person and initially think of them as a leader at least until they open their mouth! How has this come about in the U.S. culture? The answer lies interestingly in the education system and the timing of the school year, which is September. The children who are born at the beginning of the year tend to be taller and are naturally given more responsibilities by the teacher, so learn early on the art of leadership and build an innate confidence. So what happens when we meet a leader who is shorter than average? They are automatically at a disadvantage as they do not fit the cultural norm, so at the unconscious level have to work harder to prove themselves.

For the wheelchair example, considering height again, how might people talk and engage with you? As far as age is concerned, how are the older generations viewed? Revered or ignored?

So to answer the original question, yes, we do have different experiences and the frequency of these experiences dictates our reality. That reality can be positive or negative depending on your and others' perceptions and beliefs and these lead to micro inequities in the way we engage with each other and make assumptions about them. If the frequency of those experiences is more negative than positive then we become disengaged.

So as a leader, how do you know and find out whether your people are engaged?

There are a few open questions worth asking genuinely, but make sure you adapt them to your own words and ensure they are culturally respectful.

"What's happening to you that might impact your ability to make a full contribution?"

"What are you experiencing that leaves you feeling more excluded than you would desire?"

When you hear the answer, listen carefully to what is being said and not said, use the tools of rapport and connection and agree a course of action which both of you can own.

Conclusion

Why have I been sharing this chapter with you? Because I believe strongly that we need to keep in mind that inclusion is a verb and therefore we need to take action and behave as leaders if we want to create an inclusive environment. What we can do is continue to be curious and non-judgmental, which is at the core of inclusion, and also adopt the mindset of a welcoming host.

I have found that being genuinely interested in people and who they are by asking simple questions can reveal much more than just seeing them as a resource. Not everyone will want to share their personal journeys especially in the workplace, but if you don't ask simple questions, how will you know what makes people tick?

KINGSLEY WEBER

Kingsley Weber has considerable international senior management and consulting experience with major private and public sector clients, including Astra Zeneca, BP, Castrol, Carestream Health, Merck Serono, MEASAT Satellite Systems, Prince Court Medical Center and the British Foreign Office (FCO).

His work on multicultural leadership, cross-cultural connections and managing diversity by using an integrated framework to deliver inclusive strategies has helped these organizations to recognize the operational benefits of using innovation, strong leadership, culture change and inclusion to increase efficiency, output and productivity.

Kingsley joined the Pluribus network several years ago and is involved in various D&I projects as a Senior Associate.

Kingsley was born in Sri Lanka, with Sri Lankan, German and British heritage. He is a Fellow of The Royal Society of Arts (FRSA), Member of The Institute of Directors (MIOD) and Member of The Chartered Institute of Marketing (MCIM).

Baby Boomers, X, Y and Z Generations, together change agents in the workplace?

by Stéphanie Léonard

"The new generation is terrible.
I would love to be a part of it!"

Oscar Wilde, Irish writer

"Each generation imagines itself to be more
intelligent than the one that went before it, and wiser
than the one that comes after it."

George Orwell, British writer

"A generation which ignores history
has no past — and no future."

Robert Heinlein, American writer

"Every generation laughs at the old fashions, but
follows religiously the new."

Henry David Thoreau, American writer

Introduction

Nowadays, corporations are facing challenges as different generations work together. How is it different today, when companies have already been subject to the arrival of different generations at work for decades? Is this topic still relevant or is it considered "old news" (or is it instead a trendy topic, or a business opportunity for consulting companies, or for press articles?).

You might have noticed that we live in a world which evolves at the speed of a Eurostar... or even faster... The Eurostar is probably now seen as part of the past! Ten years ago Facebook didn't exist. Twenty years ago the Internet didn't exist.

Time is shortened, hours have become precise and a constant source of revenue, such as at high trading frequencies, for which time is measured in nanoseconds. Today, information can circulate around the world in a split second. This immediacy has resulted in an automatism to reply to an email the minute or within the hour it is received, or to wait for a response from one in that same timeframe. The border has now become the world itself, and new technologies continue to give place to new work opportunities.

The last 20 years have revolutionized the diagrams and the systems, but have we individually and collectively followed the movement? Is this rapid change of one's point of reference the source of this topic?

When I lead workshops around the topic of Diversity & Inclusion or even when I coach heads of corporations, the subject of age captivates as much as it irritates. If we take a look at facts, in France for example, age is one of the top three factors of discrimination.

We certainly don't know what the future will bring, but one thing is certain: the future emerging in our daily lives today requires agility and flexibility. For corporations, the challenges are the following: new employments, new markets, internationalization, and new communication techniques. So how do companies lead three generations who relate to different models or representations of the world and of the work relation?

In order to move from "denial" to "integration" of the fact that three to four generations cohabit together in the workplace, human resources departments, directors, managers and collaborators will tend to stroll through this topic all the while searching for key readings, sometimes at the risk of focusing on categorical analysis packed with stereotypes and prejudices, and therefore discrimination.

So how can we act upon this to make sure Baby Boomers, X, Y and soon the Z Generations become agents of the changes in the workplace?

The needs and risks of categorization

Challenges and Fears

Faced with the stakes of market internationalization, the rapidity at which information circulates, and the ever-growing competition, companies nowadays must be agile and flexible. Any innovation, even if simply created in a garage, urges and incites them to adapt themselves rapidly. For that matter, they will have to rely on their strengths, such as their human resources departments, to live up to performance challenges within a short timescale.

Subsequently, the fears that emerge are more than the fear of failure, which would in this instance be rapidly resounding and visible. In fact, the real substantial fear is to miss out on innovative technology, which could have led companies to seize business opportunities or expand their market shares, and therefore gain profit and further develop their business.

Consequently, directors, HR personnel and managers will attempt to adapt to make their company agile in order to face those challenges. What will be placed under reconsideration will be the system, the production tools, the company costs etc. It will be about researching the renowned ROI (return on investment). We are then quickly faced with the men and women who constitute the company. But do we have the correct and adapted human resources for these challenges?

This need for references and clear understandings will lead companies into researching various studies, statistics and facts that will enable them, if not reassure them, to identify the people who could support them in the growth and performance of the company. In these studies, we will find information, numbers and characteristics of the current generations present in the workplace.

The generations

So, what are the key aspects of these studies? What are those generations that work in the industry today? What do we read about these generations? They are described by a context of key events and key characteristics, notably relating to their relation to work.

Baby Boomers (1943-1964) – achievements at work

Key events:

- The Second World War and the peak of post-war births

- The economic renewal, notably in North America

Key work relation characteristics:

- Entry in the job market with exceptional employment possibilities

- Life centered on work and the social values linked to having a career

- Respect of authority and the hierarchic structure

- The feeling of belonging to a corporation: collaborators considered as part of a family, a "job for life"

Generation X (1965-1980) – searching for challenges and the need to learn

Key events:

- Social transition: from the decline in the colonial imperialism to the fall of the Berlin Wall (which marked the end of the Cold War)

- Repetitive economic crises, difficulty to find stable work with good wages

Key work relation characteristics:

- Trust toward the corporation with which they are attached

- Respect of the hierarchy, with having to prove themselves at the start

- The ones who put into place the processes and rules that apply today in organizations

- Work seen as a place to blossom, to search for challenges, to learn, to self-develop and to experiment; the salary is not the primary motive

Generation Y (1981-1995) – coaching and feedback

Key events:

- Have not known the world without AIDS

- Generation that "fell" into technology straight from birth

- Since a young age learned to live with invading medias: TV, phone, internet and later on in their early teens, faced with the emerging world of TV reality shows and "downloading"

Key work relation characteristics:

- Balance between work, family and leisure

- Lack of understanding with regards to the need for punctuality, traditional courtesy, wearing a uniform etc.

- Independence toward the employer: the company has to be offering something, and not the other way round; they need to make their eyes sparkle

- Searching for pleasure in the workplace: a certain rhythm and fast results, a stimulating job and no routines

- Respect toward a person who can become a model; in need of a coach or a mentor, not a superior

- Constant need for feedback

- Will to reach higher levels at fast speed

- Desire to evolve within a "collegial" atmosphere, a community; valorizing teamwork

In conclusion, would the Y and Z Generations, the "hyper-connected" be the only ones that could adapt themselves to the new conditions of the market and its new challenges? How can they be better "managed" even when they "contest" the existing models and seem distanced from a certain conception of work and its work relations? Are the Baby Boomers and X Generations "out" of this economical world even though some will still be in the workplace in the next 15 to 20 years?

Age diversity: biased mechanisms and recognizing differences

How can we expand on the topic of age diversity in the workplace and go beyond appearances in order for each generation to be a part of this change? There are two steps for this:

1. Gaining individual awareness of one's biased mechanisms.

2. Knowing how to recognize and value differences and how to optimize them for the better.

Let's come back for a moment to these generations: even if the diverse and various studies have shown a great amount of information which proves to be globally true "in general" and enables us to shed some light on the behaviors in the workplace, they still remain biased ideas and stereotypes.

I will now share a few key observations on my own process:

- *My first observation* as I write on the subject for this chapter is that the dates that confine these generations differ from one source to another, including certain characteristics.

- *My second observation* is that I struggle to recognize myself among my own generation, to the extent that I am searching for new sources!

- *My third observation* is that I get the impression there are more resources and studies on the Y generation at my disposition than any other generation.

Here are a few examples of my own biased mechanisms:

- Biased regarding confirmation of hypotheses: I prefer elements that confirm rather than those that revoke.

- Biased regarding representation: I consider one or certain elements as the representation of a population.

- The auto-stereotype (P. Scharnitzky): the group I belong to seems to me more heterogeneous than the other groups (aka the "other generations to which I don't belong").

The conditions that could lead to a stereotyped mechanism need to be clarified. Among these conditions we will find in particular:

- The pressure of time and results: our goal is to act fast. In a challenging economical context where we need to react the quickest way possible, the trap would be to take shortcuts. Example: to privilege a certain generation instead of another for certain functions while occulting the individual skills evaluated.

- Fear/Stress: we must act fast but also do well and provide high standard results. Therefore, we also have the tendency for the need to be reassured. A way for this will be to find "rational" or quantified elements, which will make it possible to support one choice rather than another.

A first step toward an intergenerational industry and toward all other diversities will therefore be to challenge our own reasoning and to observe our personal process. To go further and to surpass this first step, it is advisable to continue the learning process with readings and by extending our curiosity.

An example? Among all my research, an article particularly retained my attention: "Do generations maintain a different relation with work?" by Dominique Meda and Patricia Vendramin (original French title: "Les générations entretiennent-elles un rapport différent au travail?"). Based on European research, this article gives an account of the transformations of the relation with work in an intergenerational perspective. It discusses particularly the engagement of young Europeans at work.

In addition to giving numerous keys to comprehension, a particular argument in this European study stuck with me: the younger generation globally grants as much importance to work as the older generation (61% for Generation Y, 67% for Generation X, and 53% for Baby Boomers). Here is a splendid trait the generations have in common and which rather demystifies the importance of work between the generations – particularly Generation Y who sometimes have the etiquette of being disengaged at work!

All the studies available are certainly good for points of reference; they are necessary to decrypt the topic but don't suffice. They might even be dangerous if, for example, they influence employment, whether internal or external, leading recruiters into thinking a certain generation is more adapted than another for such jobs, such functions, and such challenges.

Beyond gaining awareness of this process, the interest is to continue this fabulous adventure toward diversity. The revelation of The Developmental Model of Intercultural Sensitivity by Milton Bennett is an example of something that will help us progress and go from "denial" to "integration" via "inclusion": in short, to go from a position of resistance to a position of openness.

Dialogue: source of intergenerational links

Does the particular argument in the study asserting all generations in the workplace give the same importance to work give us a lead that allows all these generations not only to work together but also be change agents, and support the new economical models that are emerging?

The substantial successes and breakthroughs that come out of a D&I workshop are often found simply through dialogue and lapses of time conversing and holding exchanges. Workshops are composed of participants from all three generations that have in common at least the place they work at. The finality of this exchange has a double effect: it enables people involved to share their points of view on the common subject of the work relation, as well as discuss the thematic questions of what they've experienced in a professional context.

The aim is to offer at the same time a space for listening and a space for expression (where words can be heard or spoken) and to put forward an environment where one can speak effectively on the difficulties or the successes that come across in this particular problematic.

A facilitator will put in place ground rules to allow for quality time of conversation and discovery, which will enable participants to challenge the visions and stereotypes induced by studies and medias. Therefore, the link created leads to mutual enrichment, the removal of biased thoughts and the capitalization of any previous ideas. There are a few necessary conditions to guarantee this success: open-mindedness, respect, suspension of judgment, generous listening and confidentiality.

One thing is certain today: the necessity for each and every one of us to be agents to our own development, and that is whichever generation we belong to. The creation of a culture of inclusion is an indispensable condition to allow at the same time awareness but also the expression of one's talent, whatever age or professional situation.

To conclude, as a facilitator of Diversity & Inclusion programs and workshops for various companies, my biggest preoccupation is to shed light on all the subjects of diversity within the workplace, with studies assuredly, but primarily by putting forward the common traits that will allow us to develop an inclusive culture.

Is an inclusive culture that allows everyone to value their similarities and their differences not the ideal answer to the challenges in the workplace? We have this conviction at Pluribus!

Charles Darwin said: *"It is not the strongest of the species that survives, nor the most intelligent that survives. It is the one that is most adaptable to change."*

STÉPHANIE LÉONARD

After having had a rich and busy career of 18 years in the sector of recruitment, Stéphanie founded Aimotion.

As a certified coach and trainer, she offers a full range of services for men and women in career management. Her effective and alternative approaches based on systemic coaching using collective intelligence processes and dialogues allow her clients to revitalize their professional careers in tune with their personal values.

Her passion is to help women and men to model their professional activities as a source of well-being.

Stéphanie has been working with Pluribus as a Senior Associate for several years, assisting global clients to value diversity and create a culture of inclusion.

Stéphanie is 45, married to Gilles and based in Paris. They have a 14-year-old daughter, Margaux.

Drive innovation through more inclusive employee engagement

by Daniel Stane

In today's global organizations there are few compelling and sustainable differentiators besides the talent and contribution of employees. When it comes to looking at the make-up of their workforce, many organizations have come to realize that diversity is much more than a statistical issue of age, race or gender. Understanding the true diversity of your people means recognizing **all** the ways in which employees are similar or differ. This could be their geographic location, cultural preferences, personality, grade or experience – among countless other aspects of diversity that could be affecting levels of engagement and performance.

When it comes to an organization's ability to innovate, the way different individuals think about their work – known as "diversity of thought" – merits as much consideration as any other difference. Like personality and cultural differences, diversity of thought is often not clearly apparent or visible; yet, its impact in terms of a richer flow of ideas can have a very tangible impact on our ability to solve problems effectively, serve customers and compete.

Arguably, diversity of thought is the most powerful way in which we are different, as it is the culmination of everything we learn about ourselves, our families, our cultures and our world as we grow up. Each of us has experienced a unique set of interactions with people, places and things, and different methods and speeds of processing information. How we absorb and process these interactions determines who we become, as this drives our thinking and, subsequently, our behaviors. The continually evolving or reinforcing effect of our experiences on our thoughts creates our "world view," the unique lens through which we interpret the world and process information.

When this inherent diversity of thought becomes recognized and valued in organizations, it can lead to both a shift toward greater appreciation and inclusion of all aspects of diversity, and a culture that stimulates unprecedented levels of creativity and innovation.

The idea of increasing performance through improved employee engagement is therefore just the start. In our experience, organizations that evolve their culture with a commitment to the inclusion and engagement of **all** employees can begin to overcome obstacles that have previously prevented certain groups and individuals from feeling both included, and that their unique world views and contributions are sought after and valued. They can also find the answer to many a critical strategic challenge e.g. how do we (begin to) meet the evolving needs of our markets; rise to rapid technological advances; better understand new client and employee segments; and get closer to responding to the emerging future without over-relying on a narrow and potentially outdated set of internal world views?

There are three key hallmarks that these successful organizations share which, in our view, have enabled them to demonstrate this true commitment to inclusion in a sustainable way and thus be able to leverage diversity of thought across their workforces:

1. Commit to the development of **all** staff

2. Uncover people's hidden strengths and personal drivers

3. Build "innovation trust" and confidence in your teams

As we elaborate on each of these hallmarks below, we will add some specific mindsets or strategies that our work with these organizations has helped develop and which, over time, have become important "engagement enablers." These are practical and effective approaches that are consistently strived for, modeled and practiced by all leaders and their teams in order to be able to achieve sustained levels of enhanced engagement.

1. Commit to the development of all staff

We have noticed a clear link between an organization's desire to promote learning across the board and its capacity for market-beating creativity and innovation. Organizations with the policies and committed leaders in place to deliver on growing the talents of all employees, not only the "talented few," reap the rewards of improved performance from colleagues who feel more engaged as a result of their individual capabilities and potential being actively utilized and developed. To succeed at this means a considerable cultural shift toward shaping an environment where everyone in your organization (management and non-management) subscribes to a way of thinking that supports the development of all.

In terms of actual investment in employees' professional development, organizations that stand out here prioritize this for all employees, regardless of performance level or rank; this gives everyone the chance to maximize their potential through relevant and impactful training, coaching and mentoring. They also push the boat out when it comes to supporting employees to work for longer term qualifications. UPS for example, do this through their Earn & Learn program, offering financial assistance to part-time employees to study and accelerate their progress into full-time and higher paid roles.

Enabler 1: Develop your people believing that everyone can be successful

When managers believe that most people have enough raw ability to be successful, they can focus their attention on always better understanding their strengths and unique potential, and then supporting them to build their confidence in the most appropriate way. However, when it comes to selecting colleagues for critical "on the job" development opportunities or stretch assignments, many managers will choose someone who they feel comfortable or some affinity with. Why? Because it's a pretty natural human reaction to do so – especially when you consider the extra energy you need in order to work with someone who is different in a way you feel less comfortable with. As a result, it is not surprising to observe many similarities between managers and their typical "go to people" along the lines of gender, age, communication style, interests or ethnicity. There's no need to feel bad about our human tendencies to favor certain people in this way. However, whether they have been conscious or not, it is worth noticing the impact such preferences or biases have on our colleagues' and organization's ability to succeed.

When it comes to development conversations, it can be challenging to have an effective conversation about opportunities for improvement with someone you find it more difficult to relate to, or simply don't know very well. But if you do not manage your attitude and reactions around this type of discussion, differences in viewpoints or lack of true relationship and trust will take from any chance of a constructive conversation that uncovers and develops talent.

With awareness about the basis of our reactions or blind spots, and some skills to help us, it is quite possible to set a positive and productive tone. By identifying the extent to which each employee is diverse, and thus able to provide a unique contribution, managers can fashion development opportunities that leverage individual traits in line with company objectives.

This is not as easy as it sounds and requires managers to invest time in relationship building, initiating new conversations about what each employee has to offer and is interested in, and how they will progress.

Enabler 2: Clearly communicate standards and developmental feedback

Leaders and managers who want to ensure that all employees are putting their effort into what's important to the business must take the time to think through and communicate clear expectations to them. This makes sure that everyone is clear about the standards of performance required and allows managers and peers to provide specific feedback in relation to these standards.

When managers come from a belief that most people are capable of meeting a standard, any data that suggests someone has fallen short can be taken in a new context. Rather than seeing a missed target as an indication of a person's potential or worth, it is merely a new opportunity for developmental feedback.

The capability to provide strong developmental support for everyone, regardless of who they are, is a learnable skill. The investment made to provide this capability among the leadership within an organization provides the basis for consistently exceeding standards and allows quality and innovation to surface more readily.

Your key role as manager and coach is to support employees to develop a strategy for improvement and stick to it. Together you can then agree an improvement plan in relation to the original standards and goals set, ensuring this is aligned with a good understanding of the individual's current strengths, weaknesses and relevant diversity dimensions.

Adopting a coaching style of leadership (as defined by Daniel Goleman in his HBR article *Leadership That Gets Results*, 2000) where the focus is on the development of a colleague, can be one of the best ways of ensuring "mistakes" are allowed to become the best opportunities for creative learning, and people feel accepted, encouraged and supported to share their ideas and perspectives, no matter their differences.

Enabler 3: Encourage employee felt responsibility

It is critical for managers to take the time to ensure that every new assignment is positioned so that it challenges the individual and encourages them to learn in the process. This, together with the quality of support a manager provides along the way, will have a major impact on a colleague's rise in confidence and ultimate success at work. The better the support, and the more opportunities to learn, the greater the commitment in return as individuals become more determined to reap the rewards of this investment both for themselves and the organization.

For this equation to work well employees also need to be encouraged to take responsibility and:

- feel that it is their job to learn about the business **and** improve it

- understand how their responsibilities link to the organization's goals

- ask for assignments that promote the growth of a range of relevant skills

2. Uncover people's hidden strengths and personal drivers

In organizational cultures that are increasingly "flat" or matrixed we often hear from managers and their reports about their frustration in being unable to offer promotions or progressions to enough of their staff. Recruitment freezes often lead to the same symptoms. In such situations leaders can claim that their hands are tied in being able to develop and nurture a more balanced pipeline of talent. What they often miss is the opportunity to uncover colleagues' unseen strengths, explore how these can be brought to the fore, and in so doing help bring renewed motivation and discretionary effort.

How long has it been since you last discovered something new about a colleague's dream, or preference of ability? Treating each of your employees as a unique reservoir of multi-layered strengths and talents allows you to continue to find new gems within. Doing this in a consistent, respectful and inclusive way will encourage creative and diverse thinking, and result in a wider range of possibilities that can help push your team or organization past your competitors.

Below we continue our engagement enablers with some suggestions about how you could channel the kind of interesting, intriguing conversation that will get colleagues thinking differently about their work and feeling more engaged.

Enabler 4: Find out what's behind people's preferences

You may know what tasks or projects individuals in your team like to do, but do you know why? The answer can take you to the heart of a colleague's motivation and fulfillment. With this kind of knowledge you can match the characteristics of a project more closely to the fundamental needs and strengths of the person. For example, your colleague may have enjoyed a research project you set them. Rather than assume it was the research process they enjoyed, ask them to tell you. You may find they have a particular affinity with the product or market they were exploring. If so, rather than just another research assignment, their next project should – if possible – link to these products or markets. On the other hand it could have been particular colleagues or stakeholders they enjoyed collaborating with previously and, with your input, they could be encouraged to work with again.

Enabler 5: Ask about the 'big dream'

As busy managers and leaders, we often shy away from the biggest questions, and especially so with colleagues and team members who we do not feel a close affinity to. In my experience, managers can experience some fear in asking these questions and worry about their colleague asking for something they could not support them with, and whether that would mean they were a bad manager or that this is not the right company for them?

With a view to finding new ways to engage your colleagues, we recommend asking the "big dream" question from time to time; it goes along the lines of: "If money were no object or you could wave a magic wand and be in the ideal job or career, what would it be right now?" Let's say they always fancied being a tour guide, for example. Rather than dismiss this as an irrelevance to their role, perhaps there may be some way of including them in international projects, or asking them to plan an offsite event that involves taking in an interesting new location. This will provide some taste of the dream and may raise their level of engagement from restless and fearful to more valued and even inspired and willing to try something new.

Enabler 6: Turn praise into a coaching session

When a colleague is successful, a conversation that stops at mere praise is a missed opportunity. Instead, talk about the strengths behind the accomplishment. Ask how she did it and what she liked best about it.

Then ask the question: "What else went well?" at least a couple of times. This will encourage your colleague to go past the first answer and dig deeper, coming up with an answer that is potentially more meaningful to her. Stay curious, persist with the questioning and you can open up the possibility of landing on insights that can be transferred to other tasks. Depending on the outcomes you could go on and ask this person to present their approach and techniques to other colleagues. This works particularly well with high-performing colleagues who may rarely get asked to reflect on what they do well.

We also recommend expressing insights about a colleague's way of working as part of their formal performance evaluation. Articulating "how" a colleague gets results will help identify other projects that require these talents. It will also show that you are truly interested in, and understand, the value of their contributions and their individual way of achieving results.

3. Build "innovation trust" and confidence in your teams

Although the return on investment for diversity of thought stems from a truly engaged and empowered workforce, organizations only succeed here when they can fully leverage employees' belief in their own capabilities. We have all experienced the feeling of being excluded or misunderstood and the resulting negative impact on our confidence and desire to contribute. Conversely, when we feel truly empowered and confident it means we are often willing to dig deep for those great, innovative contributions.

Employees in an organization that welcomes all points of view are more comfortable expressing their perspectives without fear of negative consequences. If people don't trust the environment or team they are working in, they are less likely to raise their heads above the parapet with new ideas or suggestions they feel enthused by. Without such energized ideas, organizations will fail to adapt to the fast-changing needs of the marketplace and maintain their competitive advantage.

Engaging in innovative behaviors involves being prepared to step into some sort of vulnerability or risk. Most people's willingness to make this kind of effort will be affected by the reaction and behaviors they believe they will encounter as a result.

Research conducted at the Institute of Work Psychology on the role of trust in the innovation process (Clegg, Unsworth et al., 2002), looked at the notion of "innovation trust" which suggests people are more likely to make efforts to innovate (by creating ideas and helping implement them) when they can expect reasonable and positive responses from others. Their results suggested that people are more likely to get involved in the innovation process when they believe their ideas and suggestions will be listened to, and that they will share in any subsequent benefits that accrue.

Enabler 7: Create a safe environment for ideas and learning to flourish

Building an organization in which everyone feels free to share their thoughts and opinions isn't always easy to achieve. But it's worth the effort. Encouraging employees to welcome other points of view can drive innovation and promote an inclusive culture.

Just like trying out a new skill, for anyone to risk expressing a bold and unusual idea, they need to know they will not be criticized or laughed at. Rather, that trusting and supportive colleagues will help them refine and progress their ideas.

Think back to any situation where you have needed to climb a steep learning curve and relied on a trusted coach or team. A need for trust in such a relationship increases the more exposed you are to some sort of risk of failure, injury or embarrassment.

I recently experienced this when I decided to have my first go at flying a glider plane. On arriving at the airfield, I was overcome by an overwhelming feeling of fear. It wasn't until I experienced the professional, calm and reassuring style of our instructor that, in no time at all, I was having a go at being in charge of the controls and swooping through the air having let go of my fear enough to enjoy the experience.

Similarly, employees in an organization or team working in new or unfamiliar surroundings will gain trust through commitments honored between their manager and close colleagues. As trust grows and the need for caution lessens, they feel more confident in one another and able to take purposeful risks for the sake of achieving common goals. Trust becomes reflected in the ability to bypass certain rules and procedures in favor of trying out new ideas, sharing knowledge and deepening shared experience.

Sounds great doesn't it? Yet leaders often face the challenge of confronting deeply ingrained norms that can stigmatize failure and inhibit further experimentation. The key need is therefore to overide these barriers by creating a safe environment where people know they will not be punished or humiliated if they speak up with ideas, questions or concerns. Biases or ideas we have about people's differences, or our perception of their biases about our own abilities, are frequently the key perceptual barriers to feeling this safety.

To foster an environment in which employees feel comfortable expressing their perceptions openly and honestly, encourage all employees — from senior leaders to new hires — to acknowledge and accept ideas and opinions that are incongruent with their own. That does not mean they have to agree; it means they have to listen and accept, perhaps agree to disagree. At no point is it acceptable to put forth the sentiment that any employee should not be heard because of a variance in opinion.

It is natural to have a knee-jerk reaction in disagreement. But leaders should encourage employees to pause and listen when they hear a different perspective. Teaching employees to take a moment to consider the value of another opinion shifts the focus away from whether the divergent opinion is similar to one's own to whether it merits further consideration.

Enabler 8: Encourage relationship and a culture of positive encouragement

The most innovative organizations are usually led by skillful people leaders who actively encourage their teams to take the time and space to get to know one another, and role-model this in their own interactions. Deeper interpersonal connections and a greater sense of trust help colleagues to understand what their teams can really offer. Information and ideas are then more likely to emerge, and flow to where and when they are most needed, e.g. the fuzzy initial phases of idea generation, or at the latter more rational stages of commercialization.

DANIEL STANE

As an expert in inclusive leadership and diversity, Daniel is a sought-after facilitator, speaker and coach. He has over 15 years' experience of creating and delivering leadership and organizational change programs focused on raising employee engagement and innovation.

Daniel has worked with Pluribus since 2012 as a Senior Associate on major projects for global clients in the fields of technology, financial services, pharmaceuticals and manufacturing. He brings a deep interest and understanding of how to improve gender, generational and culture balance through awareness of individual and corporate unconscious bias, and building a more mindful and sustainable approach to leadership and decision making.

With over 20 years' of business experience, Daniel draws on career success as a senior commercial leader in one of the world's largest multinationals. Having worked with leaders from over 60 different countries, Daniel himself is bi-cultural having been born into a Czech family in London. He is married with two children.

Moving abroad and the potential impact on myself and my family

by Alan de Bruyne

Whether it is moving from one country to another for a professional reason, moving for personal reasons like marrying a foreigner and taking residence in their country, or pressured by external factors like security reasons, migration has a tremendous impact on us and on our family.

In the professional context, the good news is that most companies are aware of this challenge faced by expatriates these days and offer programs to facilitate this change. These programs are mostly focused on the material side of the transition and on the integration of the person who works for the company.

But we cannot underestimate the impact an expatriation has on a family. In this chapter we will go deeper on that aspect because we all know well that there is a direct link between the performance of an employee or manager and her or his well-being.

Potential phases we can go through during expatriation or moving abroad

First of all I would like to share a model about the phases we go through when we migrate. Keep in mind that models are most of the time generalizations and that life is more complicated. But it can help us to understand and to frame certain movements we go through.

Whatever the reason for the migration, most of us are very excited in the beginning. It gives new opportunities, saving our lives, congregating with loved ones, big expectations… We are hopeful, we can explore. This can easily go together with homesickness because we also had to leave a lot behind us: familiar environment, safety, family, habits etc. But the excitement of the new possibilities takes over.

As time passes and we stay longer in the new culture, the enthusiasm generally wears off. "It's not such good weather, people are finally not all that friendly, the people here are so superficial, the language is very difficult, nobody understands me here, I miss home, they are so dirty, I cannot find good coffee here, they make a lot of noise, they are rude here..." Before you know it, you end up sad and frustrated.

Connecting with the new environment goes less smoothly than you thought. You feel misunderstood, strange and lonely. And you go through a grieving process for everything you left, you have to contend with homesickness. You have the blues and just want to reconnect with your old environment. This is the moment you start to plan your first visit back home (if that is possible).

You are in an emotional valley. This phase is a dangerous phase, you feel alone and isolated. And even if you are there with your partner and with children, it does not mean that your partner and children are in the same stage at the same time. Others may still be in the euphoric phase, or have this depressed period already behind them and are in the next phase.

From this phase on, you have three options.

1. Assimilation

You pick up your courage and decide to merge as fully as possible with the culture and environment in which you have arrived. You observe and imitate your new surroundings, and try as much as possible to forget your own culture. You also avoid contact with people from your own original culture, because you want to move forward. This is your new life and so you decide to go for it fully. You learn the language, eat the food of your new surroundings, make new friends in the new environment, working with them, dressing like them, doing like them. The literature calls this "assimilate" or "adapt" and it seems to work: you feel much better and you're proud of your new status.

In the long run there is a great danger in this assimilation: we cannot deny our roots forever. You cannot forget yourself. You can take on a role for a while but, sooner or later, circumstances, confrontations, disappointments or crisis moments will throw you back on yourself. And then you could ask yourself: "Why am I not invited to that party? Why do I never really feel that I am part of them? Why should I do a job for which I am overqualified? Why do they like me when I'm exotic and cheerful, but they let me down when I don't feel so good?"

These are also questions that you can ask yourself when you are not a migrant yourself. The big difference now is that you migrated, and by definition you are a minority. The temptation is big to blame all your difficulties and obstacles solely due to this new context, rightly or wrongly.

The danger at this stage is that you separate yourself and become isolated.

2. Segregation

If you are arrived with your body in your new surroundings but your heart, soul and head remain attached to your original environment, then you may end up in scenario two. For example, if you've been on vacation in your home country, and when you return to the host country you start counting the days to get back on vacation to your home country. You go and live in neighborhoods where there are mainly people from the same homeland as you, or at least from the same continent, you just speak your native language, and even cook and eat your own cuisine. You make contact only very occasionally, and only when strictly necessary, with the people of the host country. You fall back on strict values of your home country because you are afraid of losing your identity.

The consequence of this attitude is that you will never really arrive in the host country. You stand on the sideline.

The good news is that there is a third option:

3. Participation

This is the place where you actively go looking to merge both cultures. You go out and look how you can participate in this new environment. You try to connect with people from your homeland but also with people from the host country. You live in a neighborhood where a diversity of cultures and identities are present. You learn the language of the host country, and participate in the social and cultural life of the host country. You keep your own traditions, but also enjoy the customs of the host country. You don't over-romanticize the homeland, but will not idolize the host country. In other words, you choose the best of both worlds.

You feel generally good in the host country, but that does not mean you don't occasionally fall prey to moments of melancholy and that you will not face disappointments. But you are fully aware that this could also happen if you had remained in your homeland.

But participating in another culture is not that simple. There could be many obstacles in your way. The biggest is language. In order to participate in social life, a common language is a must. In some countries you can get by using an intermediate language, a language that both parties are able to speak. That depends very much on the attitude of the host country in relation to languages, and this depends on the history in general of this country and their relation with the language in particular.

Advice and tips:

Read, listen, inform yourself about the history of the country or area where you go. Not only the official version but be curious and ask and try to understand what lives in the collective mind of people about their country. Learn the language of the country you live in (or at least the basics) or an intermediate language.

Connecting as an adult in a new environment is not easy. It is rare it will come and knock on your door. You'll have to be courageous. You'll have to go to the other one and take the risk of being rejected and disappointed.

But just keep on seeing the big picture. Look to your life in your homeland and see how many people you have crossed in your life and how many of all those people became close friends. It is a long and slow process and the way of connecting with people is also very culturally linked. In some cultures the way of showing their hospitality is more oriented to take care of people while other cultures are more focused on letting you do your thing.

In this last dynamic it is harder to connect, it is harder to be part of the inner circle of people. It is literally harder to see, meet and spend time with them.

Advice and tips:

Look around you if you can do some volunteer work. This is often a way to meet people and connect with them in an informal way. And it shows without words you are investing in your new environment.

Another way is doing something for which you have a big passion, for example: playing football, cooking, dancing, and following a course in this. Because automatically you will surround yourself with people you already share a passion with, and this of course helps in the connection.

It goes without saying that the transition from phase 2 to phase 3 is important, but also dangerous; you may wallow in self-pity. To crawl out of this valley you have to be courageous, and have perseverance and willingness to take the necessary action. But again, going to the other one, to the unknown requires a large dose of courage: you take the risk of being rejected or encountering misunderstanding or denial. Nevertheless, participation looks like the best option to arrive well in a new environment.

Some people go through these phases in one year, others take five or ten years, and still others might need a whole lifetime. The rhythm may vary: we can linger long in phase one, and quickly through phase two, or the exact opposite. That depends on your temperament, personality and experience of migrating.

When you move abroad as a family, we all go through these phases but all on our own rhythms. The woman who was given a promotion in her company and moved to this new country may participate very quickly thanks to her new environment. For her partner it will probably take more time, while their children move in very easily.

These different rhythms of going through these phases can create a lot of tension in a family. Especially when we are not aware of them, some of us can become impatient toward the other ones. Knowing this model can help to be kinder with each other. As I said, migrating has a huge impact on us.

Advice and tips:

- Verbalize to each other the different phases

- Look after yourself and your family members and be kind with each other

- If possible (depending on age) be sure to involve your children in these conversations

The impact of growing up in two cultures

For children it becomes even more radical. We all know how important stability is for the healthy growing up of a child. But that does not mean children cannot handle migration. On the contrary, children are very flexible and moving abroad can open their world and perspectives, which prepares them better for the more and more globalized world we live in.

But as a parent you have to be aware that the fact that your children grow up in another culture will have an effect. And again if you are aware of it instead of seeing it as an obstacle it becomes an added value. When we bring up our children, it is natural and good that we pass on values, traditions and habits that we received from our parents/culture. I am not so much talking about what we tell our children but more about how we live our lives with them. Cultural values and habits are giving through most of the time completely unconsciously.

But when we live abroad, we should be aware that our children will pick up values, traditions and habits of the new culture. They live in another culture, they move through it on an everyday basis and most of the time they will pick up completely unconscious values and habits of the other culture. Like all of us, we are a product of the era we grew up in.

This sounds logical and easy but it is not always in daily life. Children sometimes get conflicted with themselves. They have two (or more) cultures to be loyal to and sometimes it happens that there are real conflicts in these values. You could almost talk about split personalities, and most of the time they start to create what I call "in-house personality" and "out-house personality."

It is a general mistake parents often make, they think they know their children very well, but you only know them in how they behave with you. Out-house they could be very different; this is also the case if they grow up in the same culture as you. But in the new society they live the "other" culture and values and habits can be different. As a parent, it is very important to be aware of that and not view it as if your child is not loyal to you. It is so hard for a child having a secret identity that could be seen as disloyal to their parents.

I compare it often with children that grow up in separate households, where the parents are divorced. It happens that parents both have their specific approach, their values and their habits. Children are flexible enough to deal with this but it can become problematic when one of the parents starts to slander the other one (openly or hidden, it does not matter, never underestimate the instincts and subtlety of children). Because as a child, you are a child of both parents, you cannot choose between them, and your internal loyalties get into conflict.

On the other hand, if you praise the other parent as a parent (even if you don't mean it 100%) the child will be more free to look clearly and have a more realistic view of the situation and can better make up their own point of view, values, etc.

Similar dynamics happen when we grow up in different cultures. When we as parents recognize the duality the child can sometimes be, it gives the child more space to find himself or herself more smoothly.

Advice and tips:

I would invite you to verbalize this with your children and give them the feedback that it is okay to feel "home"' in both worlds. It does not mean that you have to agree with the other values, but at least you should recognize the existence of it. If your child can manage together with your guidance the growing up in a duality of cultures, they will inherit the capability to function in a seemingly conflicted world. They will be perfectly prepared to deal, work, love in a world with different values and cultures and stay in their own center.

As I said in the beginning of this chapter, moving abroad has a tremendous effect on you, your partnerships and your family. With good preparation, right state of mind, and if necessary external help, it will be the most enriching thing that happened in your life and it can make you and your context a better being.

ALAN
DE BRUYNE

Quality, connecting, humor, creativity and passion are the pillars of Alan's work.

For almost 20 years, Alan has been a passionate facilitator, speaker and coach, with Diversity & Inclusion projects all over the globe. His mission is to support leaders and clients to be more connected with themselves, their environment, their visions and their teams.

Raising awareness about unconscious bias and exploring the importance of diversity and inclusion in the workplace are part of his toolbox. Clients describe him as "light-hearted yet informative, engaging and powerful delivery."

Alan joined the Pluribus team in 2008. As a Senior Associate, he is involved with most of the major global clients of Pluribus. His strategic thinking, his process coaching, his workshops, his knowledge, mindset and experience are strongly valued by everyone, at all levels of hierarchy.

As diversity is part of his personal DNA, Alan has been involved in many diversity projects throughout his life. From local social projects with all kinds of minority groups (culture, social class, age, gender, etc.) to organizing the Belgian Pride with his team for over 100,000 people.

All these commitments help him to keep a finger on the pulse of today's dynamics in society and he translates creatively these experiences in the corporate world.

Alan speaks Flemish, French and English. He lives with his partner alternating between Valencia and Brussels.

The Pluribus working model

by Jean-Marc Pujol

1. Learning about Diversity & Inclusion

1.1 Being freelance

At the very beginning, when Isabelle decided to end her career with BP and create her own consultancy to help companies on the subject of Diversity & Inclusion, I was really happy for her that she had decided to become freelance and no longer be an employee after all these years collaborating with different companies and in different evolving roles.

I had myself been self-employed for the previous 15 years and enjoyed it very much, even if sometimes it was hard to cope with. But I believe it is a real privilege to be responsible for your own self, to be in a position to decide, and to be faced directly with the goods and the bads that may come out of it.

Being freelance has always been the right choice for me, as I find it much easier not having to report to someone else and not needing to get any kind of permission to manage my daily work. In fact, to be honest with myself and with you, I must admit that I am someone extremely independent; it is not in my nature to reach out to other people, and I instinctively like to get on with what I need to do without asking for help or advice. I realize this tendency certainly traces back to my childhood and my place within our six-children household. Certain events when I was young isolated me from my parents, who themselves had to face important issues to do with my brothers and sisters, and therefore they were not able to give me their full attention and presence when I needed it. This often unconsciously forced me to cope with situations and make decisions on my own, primarily based on what I deemed was best.

One day, Isabelle asked me if I could help and do a little bit of administrative work for her. After starting Pluribus, she rapidly became involved in a few different projects, and had no more time for back office and administrative duties. She couldn't develop the business and create connections with new clients, facilitate the project *and* manage all the financial and administrative responsibilities at the same time! Of course I happily accepted.

At first I thought it would be a one-off help, but I progressively became involved with Pluribus, and initially with that particular mindset: acting on my own based on what I believed was best, without any hierarchy to report to on a day-to-day basis and without asking for advice. I had not yet realized that it was certainly a very isolated view, and one that would make me face unexpected consequences, especially once I became increasingly involved with a diversity of people.

And now, ten years later, I am still here, and I have edited thousands of invoices for a large number of countries across the world. Most importantly, I have adopted a completely different mindset and changed my work ethic. At the time, if you had told me that I would become so busy and that I would change considerably, I would never have believed you.

1.2 Being the spouse

Before I go further in my story, I need to reflect just a moment on the personal and professional life we led in the previous 15 years before the start of Pluribus. I think you have understood by now that Isabelle and I are husband and wife, and have been since 1985.

Isabelle was working for British Petroleum (BP) and had a fast and continuously developing career that kept her very busy. She was passionately involved and very frequently away from home for long periods of time.

We lived in France for many years, in Belgium the first time for eight, in the U.K. for four years, in Germany for four years and then moved back to Belgium in 2006. We both agreed at the time that I had a role to play in order to help Isabelle in her professional career. After having talked about it, we agreed to reverse the traditional role usually dedicated to the woman in the household, and I became "the spouse."

I had myself worked for different companies and, in fact, I never found a comfortable place or firm where I could see myself having a life-long career. I even previously changed the nature of my jobs, such as from hotel/restaurant business to computer services. Therefore, I was very open to this new path.

To be honest, I simply loved the new experience of being at home, and enjoyed every aspect of it. Taking care of my children, enjoying closely seeing them grow up. I also had some time to dedicate to different activities, and they were all really interesting. I had no more stress or pressure, the kind you can suffer from by working for a company.

And so, I became "the man" of the house, the "spouse," taking care of the functioning of our home and the welfare of our children. I was also doing some small-scale professional work on the side, related to my previous specialities, through the different sole trader companies I built in each country where we resided. Of course I needed good organization, but it was not so difficult to run both.

I encourage other men to do so if the occasion arises for them; it is indeed a lot of fun! I am sure a lot of women will easily agree on that too!

Back in the 90s, being then newly installed in this spouse role, I realized that the society still had a very traditional meaning of the parent's role, and it didn't seem very "normal" to be a man attending mothers' meetings at school or at other events.

I remember being in an after-school parents' meeting for my daughter's class and being the only man there, surrounded by women. The teacher, a woman who was welcoming and leading the reunion kept saying: "The mothers who want to be involved… the mothers who like to… the mothers who cannot do… the mothers should…" never a word or even an allusion to the father. Suddenly, after a certain time being patient, I could not resist and I stood up, raised my hand and asked: "Do I have to shave my beard, wear a wig and a dress so you can notice that I am not a woman and fathers can be involved too?" All the mothers looked at me at first with an interrogative look, but then they smiled.

It was very interesting to attend events and be surrounded exclusively or mostly by women, with rarely any men. Women themselves were often surprised to see and meet me on several occasions, and perhaps thought or realized the "housewife"` in this family was a man. For me, it was also intriguing in a way to be a part of some of the conversations between women about domestic topics: children and other subjects I was not used to talking about and would have probably not spontaneously thought to speak of.

Also, newsletters and other publications received at home from the schools were always to the attention of Mrs. or Miss, never including a Mister or Sir (interestingly enough, it was also the case for the BP Expat Spouse Network – always addressed to women). I was the first to mention this during parents' meetings, I even returned letters sent to Mrs. Pujol, and pointed out that men can also be involved and this should be considered in every little detail.

I was indeed very surprised that women always wanted equality between men and women, but did not apply it to a man in situations commonly attributed to women. Inclusion was not the rule at this time.

1.3 My personal revolution

Now back to the story of Pluribus. I quickly found myself communicating with several different people, clients of course, but mainly Associates who were committed to working with Pluribus. To be honest once again, with my "independent mindset" I was not really ready for that, and I did not know at the time that dealing with other people would be so difficult. I was about to learn so many things about how to work with people and about myself, little by little every day.

Pluribus soon enough became increasingly popular and recognized, and the projects grew rapidly. There were times when I got slightly lost, with so many things to think of and decisions to make within our specific organization situation: working with freelancers, all independent and dedicating a part of their time to Pluribus. Everybody wanted quick answers and sometimes it was too much pressure; I was not always ready to react the right or appropriate way, not always having time to pause and think and therefore feeling totally out of my comfort zone.

As mentioned above, my instinctive way of doing things had always been to decide alone and take action. However good or bad the result, this way I could only blame or congratulate myself, and reaching out to other people for advice or help was not a habit. So naturally, I thought this was the right thing to do when working with others. At first, I noticed that people did not agree with me and had their own ways, own ideas, and own styles of work. I was surprised and nervous because I didn't understand why they didn't like how I had done something, or hadn't just taken my advice and done what I would have spontaneously done myself. I found myself uncomfortable "in my own skin" and the reactions I received were not ideally the ones you would want to have, and to me they felt more like adversity at first.

It took me a while before I understood that everybody is different, not just by gender, but also that we can see the world through different lenses and sometimes we miss the true reality because of biased thoughts and wrong (re)actions. As you can imagine, it was not easy for me to realize this, and I was certainly not prepared or equipped for such situations. However I gradually learned and understood that everyone can have valuable advice, everybody should be respected and that I did not have the innate knowledge and the correct answers to everything. Sometimes I had to learn the hard way, by being confronted by people who clearly told me that I did not have the right attitude and that I was too arrogant.

Over the years, by being more and more involved in the company and learning every day about the many different aspects of Diversity & Inclusion, I progressively started to listen more, learned how to step back when it was needed and not to force the way, not thinking I was always right. Sometimes I was able to find quick answers that were the correct path to solve a particular situation, but I have now learned to be more patient and listen to others first, even if at the end they come up with the same solution! This helped me increase my reflection and brought even better options and solutions to the table.

I am convinced now that the most important keys to have to ensure the success of a business are trust, transparency, humility and actively sharing these same values. You must not be ashamed or uncomfortable to say "I do not know" and ask for help and advice. It will make you grow.

Transparency rapidly became a business model for us, certainly when you play the role of subcontractor and sometimes of sub-subcontractor. Today at Pluribus, at every level, every actor is aware of the main information and we share it with respect and in accordance with a confidentiality agreement.

I am now very happy to be able to react to the similar situations I was facing before with a different approach, and with the appropriate behavior. Today I feel I have gone a long way; it was not easy to convince myself that there was another possible method to act and react, and I thank our Associates because they helped me a lot by being patient and also respectful toward me.

"Walk the talk" is something I learned and try to apply to my very best now on a daily basis with our colleagues and clients. This has also contributed to having better relationships in my private and family life.

I also want to thank our clients. I learned to not let my ego conduct my spirit and, as previously mentioned, I often learned it the hard way; confronted by structure, organization and process I had to simply accept without second thoughts. The client is always right, correct?

2. Learning every day

Learning every day is a must when you believe it is good for you, and with humility it will lead to success in this field.

2.1 Relations with people who do not belong to your company

It is not easy to work with people who don't solely belong to your company but who are actively participating in the business. You can't really play the traditional boss role or enforce hierarchical authority. You first need to really care about others and be able to think outside the box. This is another thing I learned or earned on this journey. Thank you Diversity & Inclusion!

Beforehand, I was not aware that inclusion was the most important practice to apply when working with others. Building projects together, sharing ideas and decisions one step at a time, respecting different viewpoints and giving each other the platform to talk and be themselves is a powerful way to find success in our enterprise. The real power here is *listening*.

It is also a joy to value and accept someone else's idea instead of being jealous and feeling frustrated for not having thought of this idea yourself. If one does not respect a few basic rules and proactively learns and applies correct methodologies, the success of a team can become uncertain and things can be complicated.

I was lucky to be given the opportunity to open my mind and learn and access different knowledge and techniques, and this is certainly thanks to the Pluribus business model. I was quickly convinced and certain I was on the right track because I was already taking better decisions and apprehended situations with more confidence and humility, which led to better decision making and results.

Having a wide range of skills is vital for a company's economic performance. An international group should represent people from a variety of customer profiles. This is the best way to understand and satisfy. Diversity by facilitating the exchange of ideas, experiences and cultures also increases our potential for creativity and innovation for the benefit of our clients.

2.2 The Pluribus working model

For the last ten years, a lot of people have been engaged in making Pluribus a dynamic and successful organization that offers high level Diversity & Inclusion services, and advises and delivers to companies across the world.

Pluribus is an entity that regroups only women and men freelancers of different nationalities, origins and cultural backgrounds. They are not Pluribus employees, they are Associates, keeping their own business identity, but putting on the "Pluribus hat" when working with our clients.

We are all self-employed, we do not belong to the same single company, and we all have our private brand. So how is this possible, you might be asking yourself?

I think the secret is that we see ourselves as all being on the same level, with no hierarchical structure whatsoever, and we share the same values. At Pluribus, the key words are always *trust* and *transparency*.

At first, we were already confident that this model was viable but we were lacking prior experience and therefore we did not have a ready-made structure. Over the years, work processes have improved thanks to the contribution of all. It was like building a house. It is necessary to identify all the processes and ensure that they work together harmoniously.

As Head of Operations and Finance, from the beginning, I tried to provide simple and easy working tools to be used. I learned that sometimes what was easy for some was not the same for others. Also, I have been able to produce and develop simple documents to be used over time.

Because of this collaboration we were able to develop different tools that appealed to all, and each of us could claim a share of paternity in some way. Listening and sharing are essential points in this kind of business.

It is also important that every actor in such a business model can represent the organization in the same way, in order to keep a coherent image of the company and avoid confusing the client. Therefore, none of our Associates ever use their own name or brand when acting for Pluribus; everybody is provided with all branded and personalized support documents and media tools to approach our clients.

Another master word is *sharing*. At Pluribus, we understand that helping each other and sharing our point of view, experience and expertise is a must for the client. At every level of the process of a project, all the Associates involved are aware of everything and can access the central database easily to bring their contribution. Indeed, this often helps improve our work with our client who can then benefit from such positive and powerful results, but this way we can also all benefit from the experiences of others.

Of course, the financial aspects and the possible working scenarios for the clients are clearly defined, and we have built a real win-win collaboration so everyone can give and take and feel comfortable about it. Everybody can express his or her feelings and advice with total transparency.

We also walk the talk. We could not advise our client around Diversity & Inclusion themes if at Pluribus it was not a daily practice at every level of the relationship and organization to process our mission and projects.

We had to decline a few projects or offers because we did not feel that the prospective clients were really and deeply engaged to share those values with us, and it is so important to bring the right and successful impact to a project.

Diversity & Inclusion is so specific that it cannot be just a "tick the box" action. It is a long journey with no beginning or end that we have to embrace together with our clients, with patience and humility, to be able to achieve positive and tangible effects for the companies we share a partnership with.

And so here is probably another key to success, no need for big demonstrations to convince people – just walk the talk!

I also have to admit that certain types of people are not able to join an organization like Pluribus. We have faced one or two cases throughout our journey and these people ended up leaving by themselves, as they are not able to honestly join and practice our core values of sharing and respect, the pillars of our model.

2.3 Learning from our clients

Throughout these ten years working at Pluribus, I have been directly involved with the procurement process for the companies we have worked with.

Sometimes it has been easy, sometimes complicated; the larger the company, the larger the binding financial and administrative procedures. It is the same for the offers prepared that we put forward.

Even if this was quite complicated at first, it became a rewarding experience that has allowed us to grow and learn many more things.

So thank you to all our customers for this but also for their trust and all the opportunities encountered and exchanges that are still very rich today.

3. Becoming a better person

In the past, I was not the best person to work with, but I did not realize it at the time. As I have stated above, it was not easy at first for me to take part in an organization with such a specific business model.

However, over the years, with the various confrontations I have had on a non-hierarchical basis and with people who knew more than me on the subject of Diversity & Inclusion, it has altogether turned out to be a real blessing.

It took time, but now I realize that I am more flexible when approaching situations, and can view them with perspective, especially on scenarios that could test my ego and that beforehand normally would have made me react too quickly and certainly in the wrong manner.

I learned that time for reflection was healthy, and it could result in the image others have of you to change for the better. Patience allowed me to showcase another aspect of myself, and when certain people took notice of the changes in my attitudes and reactions and sometimes gave me a compliment, it delighted me and encouraged me to continue to move forward in that direction.

With this experience in mind, it is clear to me that an organization such as Pluribus can benefit you, your colleagues and also the clients. This work model gives you the opportunity to self-improve and certainly offers you the right tools for it. You just need to desire it. When the train is there, jump on it if you do not want to miss it.

Thank you Pluribus for taking me on-board and helping me become a better person. I know the journey is still long, but I am on it, working hard and enjoying every part of it!

JEAN-MARC PUJOL

Since 2006, Jean-Marc works as Operations and Finance Director at Pluribus.

Since November 2015, he also acts as a massage therapist following Ayurveda traditions.

After a degree in hotel management school in 1976, Jean-Marc started a career in the hotel and restaurant business for a big group in France and moved up to different responsibilities and sectors, ending as Food Managing Director for a major hospital in Paris after ten years. He then bought and managed his own restaurant near Paris in partnership with his wife.

After two years, due to some professional opportunities, he lived and worked in Belgium, U.K., Germany and is now back in Belgium. He supported his wife's career and took care of the well-being of his family, building different independent businesses each time, mainly in the computer services sector where he gained a diploma at the French Chamber of Commerce.

Back in Belgium since 2006, he works as an independent in the computer sector, providing services and support to families. He also takes care of the Pluribus back office and is managing full-time all operations and finances until now.

Jean-Marc is always ready for new challenges, with a strong focus and action oriented. He has been keen to develop over the years his skills to be a team player and fully support his colleagues and Associates.

Jean-Marc discovered a passion for Indian massage based on the Ayurveda medicine and is learning in this field since 2013. In November 2015, he decided to start a massage activity in parallel to his activity with Pluribus.

Jean-Marc wishes to continue to explore the Indian massage field and to practice this art in the years to come. He is also a garden lover taking care of his own flowers and vegetables. He enjoys cinema, reading books and traveling the world.

All on the same page

by Elizabeth Auzan

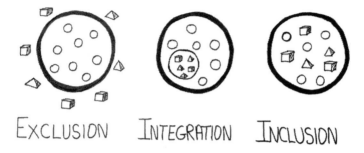

EXCLUSION   INTEGRATION   INCLUSION

When discussing diversity, it's always difficult to make an exhaustive list of what constitutes this concept. Using words tends to create rigid categories, not to say silos.

One way to overcome this challenge is to use a graphic representation with colors that are not associated with race for example. In the above diagrams, geometrical shapes represent different entities which can be interpreted in different ways according to one's perspective.

There is no suggestion of gender, race, religion, social status, physical appearance, age etc. which are typically used to categorize people. There is thus no identification, no contextualized resentment.

These entities can then be represented in different, very *simple,* graphic contexts which immediately bring home the reality of what the groups experience in social or professional situations from exclusion to inclusion. We can *see* how it must feel in the different contexts.

Images appeal to what is commonly referred to as the right brain. Although this term is not scientifically satisfactory, it points out that the different functions have been observed to be located in different parts of the brain. Functions considered as "right-brain" include creativity and intuition as well as reflex-mode actions such as taking a shower. This part of the brain looks at the big picture and conjures up images. It works very fast. The left brain deals with rational tasks based on procedures and works in a focused, linear fashion using words and is necessarily slower.

Dan Roam, in his book *Blah, blah, blah. What to do when words don't work*, deals with the power of visual thinking and compares the right brain to a humming-bird which flies over the forest and takes in the whole forest. He compares the left brain to a hungry fox crossing the forest in search of food. Focusing on one single activity and the desired outcome means that the fox sees only what is absolutely vital to serve his end.

Both sides are necessary for a balanced life and both approaches are necessary for a balanced, effective team.

In a Western-centric society, education is very focused on left-brain achievements and metrics to evaluate them. Measurable performance is the norm. The unspoken assumption is that if it is not measurable it is of no value.

This tendency creates an environment where it is assumed that there is only *one* (left-brain, logical) way to solve a problem, that there is only *one* right answer and that one must find that answer however long it takes. If one fails to find that answer then it is a source of shame and brings criticism from one's hierarchy. This, in turn, creates a silo mentality where competition replaces collaboration. It is not surprising that this environment is dominated by testosterone thereby leaving little space for women or non-alpha males and stifling creativity and innovation under compliance and jargon.

Our experience is now telling us that this environment is no longer viable in our fast-moving, hyper-connected world.

Corporate jargon has already taken this on board and we are served bland slides presentations using big words such as entrepreneurship, transparency, respect, collaboration, innovation, diversity etc. If top management is not convinced and committed to walking the talk and transforming the official discourse into concrete action then the situation cannot change.

Developing right-brain capacities through visualization techniques is one way to challenge the status quo in order to cope with and integrate new paradigms.

We have already seen in the infographic representing the transition from exclusion to inclusion how complexity can be clarified and simplified. In business schools, innovation challenges include brainstorming techniques such as the Deep Dive where visual facilitators support groups and help them clarify and express their ideas in drawings and metaphors. These drawings are then used as a basis for presentation where the *story* can be told, human to human, without innumerable and complex slides to distract the audience. Of course, this is an enormous challenge for left-brainers who feel exposed with no screen to fall back on. However, the spontaneity and presence of the presenters using simple, hand-drawn images establishes better rapport with their audience.

But clarifying and simplifying issues is not the only way visualization techniques, which stimulate the right brain, can be used in business situations.

I would like to share with you four real-life examples of visualization techniques in business situations in which I was personally involved and then explore how opening up to right-brain activities is a great way to be not only more innovative but also more inclusive.

We have often heard or used the rhetorical question "Are we all on the same page?" But what if everybody was *literally* on the same page? What if we could bring that metaphor to life?

Visualization techniques and right-brain thinking are by nature inclusive and non-gender based as I hope the following examples will show.

Graphic recording

A trained graphic recorder, standing at a wall, draws a large-scale map of the event on paper. This work evolves as the discussion advances. The resulting drawing is a source of reflection for the participants who can see, in real time, the work they have just accomplished.

For the graphic recorder, all voices have the same value so there is no pre-established corporate hierarchy. Participants feel listened to by a neutral ear. They can come and share their memories or commentaries.

I, personally, always encourage them to take up a marker and add their own comments. Possibly, people who have not felt able to voice their thoughts or who have had additional thoughts can then feel empowered to express them. The phrase "all on the same page" has been materialized. The map is often put up in the office as a souvenir or photographed and used in internal communication.

Collective painting for team-building and motivation

Imagine 120 senior managers from a global company in the same large room dressed in protective overalls and mobcaps, without shoes but feet covered in protective slippers. Hands are hidden in latex lab gloves. They come from very different parts of the world but at this precise moment there is no differentiation between sexes or status.

No one yet knows what they are going to be asked to do dressed in this way. They are on their annual retreat and have already been encouraged and coached to present their values and innovation challenges in graphic form.

Now imagine 12 groups of ten people standing in a long line in front of a 12m long, 1.3m wide sheet of paper. On the paper is a DNA structure in pale grey. Each group has one linear meter to play with. The instructions are to color in the DNA structure in blue and green and then decide collectively what the group wishes to portray of its learnings from the past two days and its hopes for the future. They are given acrylic paint, brushes, sponges and buckets of water to do so and 20 minutes to realize their "masterpiece." An artist is on hand for any last-minute technical advice.

The sheer energy and enthusiasm this exercise engendered was spectacular. People got excited, shouted ideas to each other, encouraged each other, found artistic ways of expressing their solidarity and even played around covering a hand in paint and patting others on the shoulder to leave a bright-colored handprint.

They had 30 minutes to play. Time constraints are important in this type of activity in order to avoid left-brain critical interference which blocks creativity.

When time was up and the whole group of 120 stood back to admire their collective work, there was silence as it hit them clearly and immediately that they all were on the same page both literally and metaphorically. E pluribus unum, so to speak!

An ambitious team-building exercise

After taking notes and graphically recording some sessions of a corporate retreat involving 150 people from all over Europe, I drew a large-scale (4.5m x 1.35m) graphic recording of the desired outcomes which had been expressed during a workshop. This included a visual representation of each country involved (from their own communication material), a metaphor I suggested and the remarks I had noted down. Again, there was no hierarchy in these anonymous remarks. My mural was carefully cut into 15 equal pieces that corresponded to 15 trays of white wall tiles and on which each team of ten had to reproduce a separate piece of the original drawing.

The challenge was to make sure the edges were exactly in the same place as the original since the tiles would subsequently be made into a mural in the reception area of a center of excellence. Everybody was dressed in the same T-shirts specially printed with the event name. They were given special markers of the same colors used in the original and given 30 minutes to finish the challenge. There was immediately a high energy level despite the fact that they had been working all day. Everyone was in the same boat and everyone was able to contribute to the project. And everyone had fun – and it worked! Unfortunately, for confidentiality reasons, the final mural cannot be shown here.

One of the learnings from this type of activity is that having fun while completing a serious task is not a contradiction in terms. On the contrary, it fosters engagement and collaboration and creates a more attractive working environment that is being recognized as important for workers, in particular Generation Y.

Art ateliers at IMD business school

Programs at IMD target leaders, senior managers and high potentials. There is recognition that in today's fast-changing world, exclusively top-down, left-brain approaches no longer work. There is much focus on mindfulness. Visual and creative tasks require concentration and focus that are important in the concept of mindfulness and something we have difficulty in achieving in a society which promotes multitasking.

Now, while one can sing and wash one's hair at the same time in the shower, these are right-brain, reflex-mode activities and both will be done with 100% of our capabilities even though the singing might not win us a place on *The Voice*.

It is admitted today that it is not physiologically possible to multitask left-brain activities such as writing a report and negotiating a contract over the telephone *simultaneously*. What happens is that neither activity is done 100% correctly as the brain struggles to skip from one to the other as quickly as possible. This induces fatigue and frustration because the process is neither effective nor efficient. Eventually this can lead to burn-out.

In the art ateliers, visual facilitators organize collaborative drawing exercises and painting workshops. The exercises take place in a multipurpose space with sports equipment pushed to the sides and the floor covered with a plastic protection. Participants are requested to take off their shoes, switch off cell phones and to sit on the floor. For the painting exercise they are given plastic aprons to protect clothing from the acrylic paint. The men often have problems tying the apron strings behind their backs. Most participants are apprehensive at first since they are way out of their comfort zone whatever gender, religion or nationality they are. One very overweight gentleman found it difficult to sit on the floor and so was given a chair and thus *included*. These exercises help flex the right brain. We debrief on how helpful right-brain activities can be in business if only to create focus. When asked, for example, if they have thought about emails or professional concerns during the exercise, participants are surprised to note that their concentration was such that no interference from other tasks was felt.

So, to recap, how can visualization techniques support efforts towards inclusion in the workplace?

- Right-brain activities, such as reading a graphic recording or taking part in painting activities require no prior training and do not discriminate in terms of gender or physical capacity.

- Images are universal, can simplify and clarify complex situations and open conversations and discussions between different stakeholders.

- Images invite storytelling, another universal phenomenon. While a graph gives precise, fact-based, apparently irrefutable information, a story can be adapted to the audience, made longer, shorter, more metaphorical.

- Corporate jargon is eliminated and conversations can be genuine, spontaneous, creative, human. PowerPoint effects and perfect, clip-art elements are too far removed from reality to touch human sensitivity.

- The involvement and focus during visualization activities shut off left-brain rational criticism of experimental approaches and leave space for creative innovation in the same way as a child is absorbed in a game. This capacity is absolutely independent of gender, previous knowledge or skill sets. In fact, in brainstorming, it is often the craziest idea that turns out to be the most effective.

- In order to voice ideas or opinions freely, a non-judgmental, collaborative environment needs to be fostered and including visuals helps this happen.

- Integrating visual techniques introduces the notion of playfulness into a professional context. Although every generation can profit from breaking the silos which dictate what is appropriate in a work context and what is not, introducing a more open-minded, exploratory environment can attract Generation Y talent who find traditional and hierarchical structures suffocate their creativity and independence. Generation Y can also be interpreted as 'Generation Why?' And, indeed, they certainly challenge the status quo.

Although we note that diversity and inclusion have become major concerns in the corporate world, the road from awareness or political opportunism to concrete implementation is not always smooth and easy.

Strategy statements and top-down decisions are a start. The condition *sine qua non* is commitment from all concerned, starting with top management. New recruitment procedures and communicating about opportunities can help to make sure that "right-brainers" are given a chance to show how valuable they can be in a team composed mainly of "left-brainers" but engaged in innovation.

Visualization techniques, engaging in right-brain, non-competitive activities allow diverse groups to engage in genuine conversations and collaborate with equal opportunities. However, one must not imagine that they are infallible.

One cautionary tale. A top manager brought in visual facilitators to support a team looking to find new solutions to a long-standing issue. The manager welcomed the facilitators, assured them they had carte blanche, then left, pretexting more urgent matters to be seen to immediately. The team had a great day exploring crazy ideas and drawing them out in large-scale documents.

The energy level was intense and the team was set to present to the big boss who had promised to review the work accomplished. At the end of the afternoon, he made his entrance, walked up to the pinboards, glanced at the results of a whole day's work, took a red marker and drew a thick line through most of the proposals saying they were stupid. The team was shocked and demoralized. Three people left the company within the next few months.

The moral of this story, pretty obviously, is that any visual and/or right-brain approaches to work must make sense in terms of desired outcomes and be supported throughout the decision-making chain. The activities need to be framed, prepared accordingly and be part of a comprehensive strategy. Otherwise, it is better to avoid them and at least be consistent and aligned with existing company culture. Used for purely cosmetic purposes or to appear trendy or politically correct they can backfire.

In conclusion, visualization techniques, well prepared and as part of a more global approach to exploring different ways of increasing efficiency in the workplace by including diverse points of view and experiences can be a great tool to help break down silos and develop a more collaborative atmosphere conducive to a more attractive workplace and an innovative mindset.

ELIZABETH AUZAN

Elizabeth is founder of Thinking Partner, a graphic facilitation service providing visual support for conferences, seminars, team-building events or innovation brainstormings. She also coaches in authentic presentations. She is interested in continuous learning and cutting out the blah-blah from presentations and meetings by using visuals, preferably hand-drawn, to encourage authentic communication.

She works in English and in French.

Clients include Nestlé, Deloitte, Geneva Chamber of Commerce, Medtronic, IMD, PMI. Win, ITU, Lift Conference.

Elizabeth trained as an ICF coach in 2006 before discovering the power of visualization to clarify and simplify communication as well as connect on a deeper level. Since training in graphic recording in 2009 she has helped organizations express and share ideas in visual form. She puts to good use her coaching training in active listening.

She is regularly invited to Pluribus Diversity & Inclusion workshops to capture key highlights.

Elizabeth is currently based in Lausanne, Switzerland.

Sometimes our major obstacles are just inside us, and we are blind to their existence

by Marcelo Agolti

Introduction

We are confronted many times with difficulties and situations that prevent us from achieving our goals and put us into trouble. In both personal and business relationships, we assume that it is the result of things or situations that are just in front of us or on the surface, like operational matters. Or we blame others for being difficult or complicated. We assume that the problem is out there, that we can see it perfectly, touch it. Sometimes we are so wrong!

It´s challenging to capture the pervasive effects of the unconscious bias in our lives. Most of the time, we are oblivious to some of the beliefs or stories that we are making up. They influence us in some mysterious ways in our decision-making process and interfere in how we think and behave. It is like shadows, not under our scrutiny nor our sight.

When I start thinking about the impact, I question myself about my own biases and how I am certainly myself influenced when I make a decision or when I am in a situation involving different people.

So first it is about raising the awareness of their existence. Then you can start exploring your own unconscious biases and how they can be stopping you from your goals and happiness. We are all on a journey, an individual learning journey, with several steps that lead us to transform our behaviors. We cannot address all at the same time, we need to respect *Kairos*, the God of Time, and be gentle with ourselves in the process.

I would like to share three case studies illustrating three scenarios where I worked as a coach or a facilitator. It will give you some insights on how to understand, challenge and remove, in some aspects, the effects of those constraints or boundaries named unconscious bias.

Case study 1 – challenging mental models

This is the story of a couple holding their own business activity. They are very good at what they do and both of them come from an underprivileged background. From a childhood where they nearly faced real poverty, they found themselves going through a successful professional growth. The idea that they have too much, much more of what they think they deserve and much more than they can even think they would reach from the early stage of their marriage, overwhelms them and deprives them of making decisions.

Both are very talented and dedicated professionals, but they are experiencing difficulties in showing up in public. They try to fit in in social settings, but this generates uncomfortable situations both in their family where they are perceived like the "new rich" and in upper circles where they feel invisible, worthless and excluded.

Another example is when they invested in a new high tech machine, very innovative, which makes a real difference in service and product quality. The idea of being exposed prevented them offering and marketing that machine to their clients and other people for a long time.

We had several coaching sessions in which we openly discussed these situations. They realized how much their humble origins affected their decisions and the progress of their business and personal lives.

We could identify several patterns and situations that would stop them growing and developing themselves. We explored how they could handle this. It was interesting for them to realize how looking at their situation with the lens of their social origins did generate doubts, back and forth situations all the time, discomfort, and had so much negative impact on their business, the relationship with their employees and their suppliers.

This was a filter they had to acknowledge. That unconscious bias and mental models prevented them from being more successful and, even worse, enjoying their success appropriately. The link between their social origins and the obstacles they were facing at the moment became clear. They could see the subtle links between situations in the past and in the present, the patterns, and the structure of those situations. We explored the differences between the artefacts, on the surface, and the real obstacle, their filters. The process was really powerful and healing as they could now name it and deal with it.

Case study 2 - challenging stereotypes

I was asked to provide some coaching to a manager and a union representative from a big company. At that time, these two people had not spoken to each for more than ten years.

They had a long history of misunderstanding, starting 12 years earlier when the company in which they both work was sold. During that process, they were on opposite sides of the street. They were both blind to the impact of the system. The system is a collection of elements that interact with each other over time to function as a whole. What we see as an outer sense is just the surface of a system. So the question is what are the root causes of the events or issues that occur on the surface? For example, they were convinced that their issue was a personal thing while it was indeed the systems: all people involved, the context, their move, their decisions and the role they had to play. All was part of the overall change process and they suffered from it.

We had the opportunity to explore this in the first meeting. I shared some insights about system thinking and how the systems limit our behavior and the role we take, sometimes without even being aware of it. I wanted them to look for the set of interdependencies governed by their conscious or unconscious assumptions that they made over the years. It was clear that the series of disagreements prevented them from talking to each other for ten years, and the more they were distant, the more they kept building a bad image of each other.

This was the first time I really experienced how strong the connection was between the quality of a relationship and the quality of the communication process. Without communication, there is no possible relationship and no possible way to achieve any kind of results, let alone achieve productivity and a sense of realization or plenitude, for the people involved in the situation.

The sale of the company was the catalyst for falling into the trap of the stereotypes about "the manager" and "the union representative." There were strong clichés who would signal which person should be fired, who would abuse his power and mistreat their subordinates, who would provoke fights and misunderstanding between colleagues, who would make differences between employees to generate fights and divide the groups with the intention to manipulate them easily.

So I decided to raise their awareness on how systems make us behave in some unexpected or unwanted ways and explore in what way we are free to operate.

In this particular case it was helpful to have a dialogue to ensure that both of them would understand that there was nothing personal in their issues. No one was the enemy of the other. No one wanted to hurt the other person purposely. There were some decisions to make because of their roles and objectives due to their respective positions.

Those stereotypes were reinforced by comments made by the employees about the union representatives and what they told their manager about them. There were probably some manipulations due partly to a dysfunctional dynamic. Unfortunately, this increased the strengths of the stereotypes and deteriorated the mood of the people involved, creating a very low morale work atmosphere, ultimately decreasing seriously the productivity of the sector, and causing serious damage to the company. Everybody felt that there were no solutions and they were stuck in a vicious circle.

My job was very challenging. I had the feeling I was entering a war scenario with the impossibility of creating a dialogue between the different parties. My priority was to ensure that people could talk to each other again and rebalance the relationships and challenge the existing stereotypes and assumptions which had built up over ten years.

I was able to help them realize that there was a strong connection with the difficulties they were facing at work and the negative impact on their personal lives. They needed to see all their single actions in any intervention were contributing to create the violent atmosphere. I helped them see that they were also part of the game.

I started individual sessions with respective leaders of each party. I tried to reveal features of the stereotypes they used to "see" the other leader. One day, I gathered both of them in the same room. We listed together the labels and stereotypes they used to have to judge the other person. It was highly emotional with a lot of tension and even a risk of physical violence.

I will always remember this session was full of pressure. Actually it helped them to reflect and soften. They started to have a more respectful dialogue. We were able to go under the surface and look at the reality through their respective lenses. Stereotyping is about being fixed into only one reality. You can't or don't want to see data that deconstruct our own perception. During this session I introduced the tool developed by Chris Argyris, "The Ladder of Inference." The ladder of inference is a simple model of the steps we all use to make sense of situations in order to take actions. Our assumptions shape how we see the world and how we respond to new information. Being able to walk down the ladder with them helped tremendously to clear up the situation between the two of them. A new foundation was built during this first session. We looked at some of the information and context in a more objective way and with no filter nor interpretation.

We agreed to engage the rest of the organization by running several workshops. The key purpose was to practice dialogue and build inclusion among the participants. The accumulated tension was lowering down and people started to learn new skills like generous listening without judgment.

It was a long process and it by far exceeded the expectations of all the people involved. We challenged, in several dialogue sessions, all the pieces about stereotypes, and how it affected the decisions they made. We removed the power of the mistrust based on their beliefs, and we built a new respectful and inclusive container of people working in that sector. Conversations were more open and honest. It was like they could breathe new air and could have a new beginning, even make jokes about the past.

After a year and a half, they were proud to be part of the process and acknowledged the success of increasing productivity, performance and motivation. One of them told me one day: "We learned so much about ourselves and how we were underestimating our possibilities." This was extremely moving.

Case study 3 – challenging perception

I would like to share the story of a young male manager. His key challenge was to recognize his own value and the positive contribution he could bring to a situation or a team. Despite his position and his what we can describe as successful career, he kept thinking that he was not worthy and could not bring enough added value to his team or organization. He was deeply insecure and was all the time looking for others' approval. His insecurity had several ways of manifestation.

I would like to draw a parallel between this case scenario and the relationship women might have with beauty. Beauty is not what we only see from the outside. It is also more about how women feel with their bodies or their way of being. Beauty is a judgment. We don´t all share the same concept of beauty. We can, however, perceive that some women have a sense of security, which is attractive and sensual, or a sense of self-confidence, that is not related with exterior beauty related with the acceptance of our own body and way of being. This is what magically appears in the room and this is difficult to describe or define.

It´s interesting to explore the judgment we have about the value we add, the beauty we have, and so on, all based on judgment or perceptions about ourselves, all about stories that we store in our minds, consciously or unconsciously, all about how we interpret our participation in the world, all deeply influenced by some of our experiences and mental frame of reference. We are sometimes challenged to perceive the link between the situations we face today and the decisions we take, with our own stories, the filters, the boundaries and constraints many times are here and now, are far away in time and space, we need to explore the links and the causes.

Why was this male manager looking for approval and reassurance? How did this search affect his behavior? How did he appear in front of others?

I am still working with him and in the last session, he expressed something that touched me. He said: "I feel like I am always on stage, doing a performance with an audience that is always judging me."

Imagine what is the impact of this perception on his daily personal or professional life.

If you have sometimes performed in a play on stage, you know how difficult and stressful it can be. You know that you are the center of attention with all eyes of the audience looking at you. Imagine how this attention can affect his moves, his spontaneity and his freedom, and how this is perceived from the people around him.

This is when I introduced the work of Dr. David Kantor. Dr. Kantor is an American systems psychologist and organizational consultant who developed the four-player model. This model, based on his theory of structural dynamics, suggests that in all interactions between people there are four possible speech acts: Move, Follow, Oppose and Bystand. And problems occur when individuals become "stuck" and over-use one of the four actions again and again, undermining effective communication and decision making.

I was also raising awareness about the differences to operate in what David Kantor´s theory calls "Low Stake situation and High Stake situation." The first ones are those in which we can flow with the situation, having no constraints, and a wide communication repertoire. On the other hand, in High Stake, because of the great pressure, we become disabled, clumsy, we lose our freshness and our shadows take control of the situations and generate exactly the kind of behavior or results we are trying to avoid.

We need to develop the capacity to bystand and observe when this is happening to us. What causes us to behave in this way, which story, theme, people; and recognize what´s happening in order to recover from High Stake situations faster.

It is interesting that the cause at the end is also the effect. It is what we call "self-fulfilling prophecy." It is like "beauty." People who perceive themselves as beautiful, at the end, will result in being attractive to the audience, and people who look confident at the end generate trust and confidence from other people. On the other hand, someone who feels insecure and lacks confidence might generate confusion and doubt.

The fundamental beliefs that he makes about himself and the world makes him behave in that way. I was able to reach that level of understanding with him. This was a must to remove this dysfunctional behavior.

Conclusion

Constraints or obstacles you face at the surface, sometimes are not the real constraints. They prevent you from looking under the surface and exploring more fundamental boundaries, deep beliefs that influence your decision-making process. You might not be aware of their existence but this might prevent you from reaching your goals. I shared with you two different types of constraints related to unconscious bias, two of them related with what Dr. David Kantor calls childhood stories, and the other one is about stereotypes. All cause us to misread what is happening, impeding our own judgment to operate freely and with more objective data. Both are a serious barrier toward our well-being and a major obstacle at the time to reach our goals, and our more ultimate vision: reaching happiness.

MARCELO AGOLTI

Marcelo Agolti is a senior Pluribus Associate since 2011. He is Argentinian, based in Argentina.

Marcelo is a member of the Pluribus global network and is involved in several Diversity & Inclusion workshops with key clients in Latin America.

For the last ten years, Marcelo has worked as a manager, consultant, professor and facilitator. During that time he has coached individuals, teams and organizations in the Spanish-speaking world through complex change processes, ultimately helping them to define and achieve their goals.

His model of intervention has three main axes: Systems-Thinking, Dialogue and Structural Dynamics.

Marcelo has studied in the U.S. and U.K. and currently holds an MBA as well as training in corporate finance. He is a Director of the Postgraduate Program of Human Talent Development at the National University of Entre Rios.

DropDrop Network

by Joanne Nihom

Drops fall and cause ripples that then become waves in ever-growing circles.

North, south, east, west; Bedouins, Druze, Christian and Muslim Arabs; Reform and Orthodox Jews: a mosaic of people, customs, and tastes. A mixed society, never taken for granted.

Even though I was born into a Jewish-Dutch family living in the Netherlands, Israel was always a big part of my life. The decision to move here was therefore a natural one. Almost naturally, I also became a journalist – a fantastic, challenging profession which gives me the opportunity to write about connections, inclusions, sharing, and storytelling. Where in the world is this of greater importance than in Israel? But the country is also about sadness and pain because of wars and terror attacks. Almost every single family is touched by this. Nevertheless there are people, and they are not a minority, who are able to overcome this sorrow and create something beautiful out of it. Powerful stories. Incredible stories.

I became fascinated by the cooperation between people with opposite backgrounds, like Jews and Arabs. In so many areas such as art, education, culture, the culinary arts, and medicine, they meet and work together – even in sensitive and painful areas, there is a connection. For example, a group of Jewish and Arab families who have all lost loved ones in terror attacks. They meet, they talk, they cry, they hug. They visit schools and tell their stories. It is wonderful to see how these people have been able to change hate into love and to realize that killing is not the solution. It's about living together and engaging with each other.

The message of these instances of cooperation is powerful. It is about building a future for our children and grandchildren. About living together, even with the so-called enemy.

But you will not find one of these stories in the mainstream media. You will not read or hear about them. It is as simple as that. The media leads us to believe that the world is in a constant state of catastrophe.

It was with this in mind that, together with my dear friend Marijn Schrieken from The Netherlands who has a practice in compassionate listening and communication, I founded DropDrop Network, a platform for all these stories. Marijn has traveled all over the world and discovered, just as I did, that what she had been reading and hearing from the media was a very small part of the whole truth. Over recent years our idea has developed into a concrete plan.

DropDrop Network will share these beautiful unknown stories from all over the world, not only the Middle East. To inspire, to give hope, to awaken, to share, to respect, to acknowledge, to reveal, to trust and to love through an internet magazine, a book and/or a documentary film, or any other tool we can use to share. Our focus is on connection, not war. It is about love, not hate. It is about mutual understanding; it is about you and me and about our lives. During this process we met, among other people and organizations, Isabelle Pujol from Pluribus. We connected right from the start and to this day Isabelle helps us wherever she can. What we share is our way of thinking about binding people and creating a different world.

A journey

Let me take you on a journey to a different world; let me introduce you to some of the wonderful DropDrop Network stories.

Yael and Fathieh, two different worlds

Meet my friends, the Jewish Yael from West Jerusalem and the Arab Fathieh from East Jerusalem: two separate worlds – or perhaps not! They met each other at The Interfaith Encounter Association (IEA), where Arabs and Jews, liberal and conservative, meet on a regular basis and talk in groups about issues in their lives. The IEA has about 30 groups all over the country. The subject might be religion, daily life, vacations, money, or their families. By talking about the things they share instead of those that divide them, the meetings are on a different level. "It goes from heart to heart and the results are friendships," explains Yael. "If we learn to know each other in this way, one day there will be a generation that can also talk about political issues. If you start talking about that right away the result will be negative, because you do not agree and then you are unable to listen to one another."

Over the years, Yael and Fathieh have become very close friends. "We discovered that we have such a lot in common. We talk about our problems in life, our thoughts and our feelings," says Fathieh with a smile. But there are also vast differences, as Yael notes: "I live a free life and I can do whatever I like; for Fathieh it does not work that way because of her traditional Muslim background. Her life is determined by her family and the society she lives in." Fathieh concurs: "When I joined this organization, my father did not agree. Over the years he came to understand its importance and now he is even happy about it. It takes time; changes take time."

A few years ago Yael got married. Of course, she invited her friend – but for Fathieh attending the wedding was not so simple. "I never go out alone and I had never been to a Jewish wedding before. I was scared to death. I was also afraid that Yael's family would not like me and that my traditional dress would upset them. Nevertheless, I went. Yael is my best friend and she is very important to me. But I need not have worried. Everyone was so nice, I really felt part of her family." Yael's face lights up as she continues the story. "We invited more Arab friends, it was so good, everybody was so happy. You know, we all plant small seeds but I am convinced that, one day, they will be strong trees. To learn about each other and to understand each other is the only basis for a lasting peace."

Michal and Russia, Hand in Hand

Two other women who have also touched my heart are Michal and Russia from the Hand in Hand school for Jewish and Arab children. They teach together in an equally balanced Arab-Jewish class, which is unique in Israel's highly segregated environment. Jewish and Arab citizens tend to live apart, whether in closely-adjoining neighborhoods in the same city or in separate towns within a region. There are but few opportunities for meaningful interaction between these two major groups, especially in elementary and secondary schools, which are almost entirely segregated.

Schools build community among parents, teachers and neighboring families, and they affect nearly every person living in Israel. By fostering peaceful coexistence in schools, Hand in Hand is helping to change the way Israel sees itself, and the way the world sees Israel. Michal, the Jewish teacher, says, "The first time I entered the school, something wonderful entered my heart, especially [seeing] how the teachers, Arab and Jewish alike, respect each other. We talk with each other and we listen to each other. I feel this kind of school is the only hope for us, Jews and Arabs, to live together. A lot of the problems we have are because we do not know anything about each other. That makes us afraid. The funny thing is that at the end of the day we are the same, there are hardly any differences between us. The kids are so used to being together, for them it is not an issue at all. They meet in school, they visit each other in their free time. There are outings, sometimes together with the parents. When you walk around the classes you realize that living together is possible."

"The minute I entered the Hand in Hand school I felt a different kind of energy," agrees Russia, the Arab teacher. "I come from an Arab village. Before I went to university, I had never met a Jewish person. To have a mixed school is the answer for our future. To keep on talking about how to live together does not work, nor does talking politics. When you live together on a day-to-day basis and talk with each other, something changes. When I look a Jew in the eye, when we talk about the Second World War, I can see her sadness. When a Jew looks me in the eye when we talk about the Nakba ["Day of the Catastrophe"], she can see my sadness. Then you understand why you do not feel comfortable and you can share those feelings. Enough of what happened in the past. We should live together, happily. It is not only the best way for the kids to learn and understand. I, as a teacher, also grow. I have to understand other people, it will make my own life richer. My dream? That we will have a Hand in Hand school in every village."

Suha Atrash, a life-changing experience

When no cameras and newspapers are around, other big miracles are happening. Meet dear Suha Atrash. Married with four children, she lives in Jaffa and works for the Peres Center for Peace. "I've been working at the Peres Center's Medicine and Healthcare Department for over eight years, and it's been a life-changing experience," says Suha, who runs the Peres Center's Saving Children program, for children from birth to age 16. Suha is the bridge between Gaza, the West Bank, and Israel, between the hospitals, the parents and the doctors.

"Over the years the Peres Center's Medicine and Healthcare Department has facilitated treatment in Israeli hospitals for over

10,000 sick Palestinian children. I take care of the administrative details associated with each case. I act unofficially as a psychologist and social worker for the families who I'm in touch with when needed," she says. "Most of them don't speak Hebrew and the Israeli hospital is a new world for them, which is one more thing they have to deal with over and above the worry and stress about their child's illness. I always give them my personal phone number, which they can use 24/7. Even after the treatment is completed, many children continue to be monitored by the medical team in Israel, and this unique connection between the Palestinian family and the Israeli team continues for a long time after the family returns home. The mutual respect that develops throughout this difficult experience goes a long way to changing mindsets on both the Israeli and Palestinian sides, and demonstrates the special outcomes that can result from cooperation.

"In the West Bank and Gaza, intermarriage is very common. This is why many children are born with genetic conditions like heart diseases and different types of cancer. Medical care in these areas is not good. We bring the children to Israel, help them with their visas and accompany their families at the checkpoints. Once the children are in the hospital, we stay in touch and whenever they need something we take care of it. Also, we keep in touch once they are back home. They often need special medication or have to travel again because of further operations," explains Suha. "And that is not all. Every child is accompanied by a family member who stays with the child day and night. Everything is taken care of. The world may think that over here there is only hate, but the daily reality is really different."

For most of the parents, this is the first time they have been in Israel. To make things easier, they can stay in a special room near their child's room – sometimes treatment involves many operations and takes a very long time. "At first most of the families do not want to come; they have such prejudiced opinions about Israelis.

But once they are here and have felt the warmth they receive, the entire situation changes. They become friends with the Israeli doctors and nurses and they feel at home and welcome. But there are other beautiful things about this project. There are also Jewish kids and their parents in the hospitals. They meet each other, Jews and Arabs. They start talking and learn about each other. Jewish parents bring toys for the Arab kids. Jewish and Arab kids play together, have fun together.

"Once they go back to the West Bank or Gaza, their stories are enthusiastic and happy. It even happens that the parents are upset because they do not have to come back anymore once the treatments are over. Our entire project is not only about treatment for the kids, it is a life-changing project for all concerned. What is difficult, though, is the financial side. We are always short of money. The hospitals and doctors give us special rates [for their services]. But this is not enough. We survive mostly through donations from abroad. It has made me aware of how lucky I am to live in Israel, to have healthy kids. I was never aware of it, but ever since I've worked for this project that has changed. My dream is that we will be able to continue this work, although I do not wish kids to be ill."

DropDrop Network is about personal connections. It is about heroes and angels, big and small. In the end, we are all human beings, working together.

It is time for a positive message that isn't exaggerated or naive to offset the negative, but simply because that's what real life is like. It's about mutual understanding. It's about you and us and our lives. That is DropDrop Network.

JOANNE NIHOM

My name is Joanne Nihom.

I am originally from The Netherlands, but I live since a few years in Israel.

I am a journalist and writer and write mainly about human interest.

My slogan in life: Never Forget The Rainbow in Your Life.

Embracing gender equality in the workplace

by Laura Bacci Garriga

My own experience of gender (in) equality

I was promoted to Director at the agency and member of the management team in the Brussels office at the age of 35. Right then I knew that even if the founder and, at that time, CEO of the company was a woman, I would never be able to aspire to a higher position. I had reached my glass ceiling. It felt like a very strong gut feeling, and it was somehow hard to accept when you are young and want to develop yourself professionally and have a successful career.

Especially so when both your parents are recognized professionals in their own field of work. My mother had been the first woman to get *cum laudes* in each and every degree through medical school in Barcelona. This, she knew, was the only way to get the degree as my grandmother, a widow in Barcelona in the 1950s, could not have afforded to pay my mother's studies. My mother was a cardiologist, a survivor of cancer at the age of 34, and a woman with a lot of character who, once divorced, paid for our studies (mine and my sister's) at school and through university on her own.

My father, the son of illiterate Italian immigrants with no money in Spain, had worked and studied his way through medical school in Barcelona in the 1960s and got a grant to study brain surgery at John Hopkins Hospital in Baltimore (Maryland, U.S.). Then he moved to Vermont and to Switzerland, to study microsurgery. Back in Spain, he founded the brain surgery department in the biggest hospital in Mallorca, the Balearic Islands.

I studied translation in Barcelona and then did Russian Studies and a Master's degree in Communications in London, and had landed at a brilliant job at the Department of Trade and Industry (DTI) as part of the Government Information and Communications Service (GICS) in the U.K. But I soon felt stuck in my position and left a full-time job in the British Civil Service to move to Belgium in 2000 and work for a European NGO, and then carried on to work for a European trade association.

I was over the moon when I first started working in a communications and public affairs agency in Brussels. It was a big step for me as I decided to leave my full-time job and comfortable salary package at the trade association at the age of 30 for a three-month internship in an agency with a pay that didn't even cover my apartment rental. But I was risk-averse and determined, and soon got offered a full-time job in the agency. I then got married and had a baby, and realized that I was the only female consultant with a child. Those were difficult times as I had to work extra hard to keep my job when I got back from maternity leave.

When I switched agency I realized that all my male colleagues were married and had children, but their spouses did not work or did fundraising activities. My female colleagues did have children with either husbands that worked flex time or full-time nannies at home.

It was very interesting, and now as I look back it's even funny, to see the parallelisms between myself and a male colleague who joined the same agency at exactly the same time. We shared an office to start with. Who was the first to get important client assignments? To get a corporate Mastercard? To travel to the company headquarters in London and in Washington? Who was the first to get a private office? Who was the first to get promoted? He was. I was always second. Even when I had brought in a client worth a lot of money on my first day at the agency. Even if my client account teams had high revenues.

I will never forget that annual review I had with the company HR Director. She was American but had come from the London office. She called me into a windowless office that was 2x2m² and just read out the results of my 360° appraisal. All my peers, senior colleagues and reports thought that I was too assertive, too ambitious, too direct. I left that meeting completely stunned. Where was the mention about all the revenue that I was bringing into the firm? Where were all those new clients that I had helped bring into the agency? The fact that I was the European lead for a global key account at the agency? Nowhere to be seen. I had been judged on subjective and emotional comments, not on proven facts and on raw data. It took me three weeks and a lot of mulling to get over that meeting.

Once my time in this agency was over, I changed career track and started my own company. Not an easy decision when you are the main breadwinner in the family, have a toddler and a 10-month-old baby. I continued my courses to become an accredited and certified coach and started to look for my first clients.

The first Pluribus adventure

A couple of years later, I started working for Pluribus and my first assignment was to go to the Nestlé headquarters in Vevey, Switzerland, and deliver a Train the Trainer program on Unconscious Biases to human resources professionals. Pluribus had started a strong partnership with Nestlé in early 2013. We reported to Sue Johnson, who had joined Nestlé as Director of Diversity & Inclusion in 2008, and has since left the company to pursue other professional opportunities.

At that time, the company had no formal policy on gender equality, but over the next few years began to implement a program to create a gender-balanced business. First trialed in Switzerland, the program has since been successfully rolled out to Nestlé's worldwide operations and is now a core part of the company's DNA. Sue Johnson was convinced that gender equality has a business context, and that it is not just an issue for human resources to deal with.

Getting the executive on board

Based on my experience at Pluribus of working with other companies such as Hilti and Philip Morris International (PMI), we believe that to achieve gender balance you need cultural change, and that cultural change needs to be driven from the top.

You have to kick-start the project by talking to the executive board to understand their opinions and their vision of gender equality within the business. While the executives tend to be broadly supportive of the gender equality concept as a whole, you quickly realize that communication about gender equality has to be in a language that the leadership team can relate to easily. This means setting an annual agenda of activities and creating fixed Key Performance Indicators (KPIs) to measure progress.

This is not about fixing quotas in gender equality programs. It is possible to set yourself the goal of achieving a gender-balanced company within a decade by creating the right conditions in the work environment. Remember, change takes time and here we are talking about a massive cultural change in behaviors that have a tremendous impact at all levels in an organization.

Conduct trials before global roll-out

Try it small, see if it works, make any adjustments and necessary changes, and then roll it out. This is what we recommend our clients to do. First, focus on selecting a very diverse team, department or country to try out the project with at the initial phase. This gives clients the chance to try the project on a small scale but with people from all around the world. This also helps to provide the company's Diversity & Inclusion team with an insight into some of the cultural challenges they might encounter when it comes to cascading the gender balance project throughout the whole organization, especially if it is one with a global reach.

The second step is to identify leaders in the company that have the potential to become ambassadors for the project. Work with them to explore how they can make a difference, and give them specific actions to fulfill. This is particularly time consuming as these people occupy demanding positions. Even getting a face-to-face meeting or organizing a call with them will take time!

It is also important to start looking at key markets, and to gather facts and figures which demonstrate the benefits of gender equality in your organization. Case studies should be collected and shared with the leadership to provide additional support to the argument.

Activity every day to promote gender equality

You need to create the right conditions for a project to be successful. Once you have convinced the senior leadership team with the facts and the figures, give them two to three activities they could do every day to enhance gender equality in their department, market or region. Make them accountable for those activities and follow up with them.

Another area of focus should be tackling the barriers that prevent gender equality. These might include legal and mobility policies, or rules on working from home. Take time to examine recruitment policies and succession plans to ensure that they take gender balance into account. Changes might need to be made to enhance these policies and create a level playing field for everyone regardless of gender.

Mobility is often a significant barrier to gender equality. Global organizations want their leadership team to be mobile to develop their talents and ensure best practices are being implemented consistently across the business. But for staff with families, international mobility presents a significant challenge. Who takes care of the children, older parents, and what does the trailing partner do in a new country?

When I was still at the agency, I remember telling my husband that I wanted to move to the United States to work at the company's headquarters. This, I saw, would be the only way to break my glass ceiling in Brussels. However, it was an impossible dream. He was an architect with a client base in Belgium, spoke no English and we would have had no family support with our two daughters in Washington. So we stayed in Brussels. In such cases, taking strategic steps at corporate level like establishing support services for female team members can positively enhance their career development and be precious when having to take the difficult decision to move abroad.

Gender balance training – the first step

Some of our clients began to implement a gender equality project by introducing gender balance awareness workshops. Our recommendation is always to ensure that men *and* women are involved in gender dialogues to understand and value each other's differences and commonalities.

Many of our clients are now also launching flexible work environment programs globally to help staff balance their personal and professional lives. They start by implementing the new guidelines at the head office by initiating practices such as breastfeeding rooms and parental leave for both male and female employees.

Our advice, based on best practice, is to encourage clients to work with local leadership and teams in each market to empower people to implement the gender equality policy. The high-profile involvement of the executive board also encourages people to take the initiative and support gender equal business decisions. And where and when problems are identified, the Gender Equality or Diversity & Inclusion team can develop tools to overcome the challenge.

Mentoring – a tool for success

One tool that has proven to be particularly successful is mentoring. It gives women access to an experienced male or female mentor who has a leading position in another company or market which participates in the program. Throughout the year, the mentor supports the employee in their professional and personal development through peer-to-peer coaching, seminars and networking events. At Pluribus we also have a lot of experience of working with "mutual mentoring" or "reverse mentoring" which benefits both the mentee and mentor and turns out to be a real mutual learning experience.

Be clear about benefits of gender equality

Some of the most difficult challenges for our clients arise when it comes to implementing the gender equality project in factories. Each factory is its own little world, and completely different from working with head office.

A big key to success is gaining the trust and involvement of each factory manager. This can be achieved by demonstrating to the factory plant's management team what are the possible positive benefits of gender equality to their plant, as well as by setting indicators to measure performance.

By building a sustainable base of support, creating KPIs to measure success, and implementing action plans to drive it forward, our clients are able to progress gender equality significantly in a relatively short period of time.

For other organizations that want to improve gender equality, at Pluribus we have one key message: never ever stop talking about gender balance. Otherwise there is no responsibility and there is no action.

Taking it further

Since then, I have worked for other companies in their challenge to embrace gender equality. From packaged goods to telecoms companies to pharma. And I am convinced that as well as creating a better pool of talent, gender equality ensures that a range of different views and perspectives are taken into account when business decisions need to be made. That includes every level of the business, from the operators in the factories to its executive management.

As far as I'm concerned, implementing gender equality measures will not only benefit companies, it will also help future generations. Girls like mine and young women from all over the world will have access to jobs and professional opportunities that neither my mother's nor my generation have even dreamt of. And this will be good for businesses, for the society, for families and for mankind as a whole.

LAURA BACCI GARRIGA

Laura is a coach and facilitator, specializing in the areas of Strategy Development, Team Performance, Employee Engagement, Communications, Leadership, and Diversity & Inclusion. She joined the Pluribus network a few years ago as a Senior Associate.

She has strong experience in designing and facilitating a wide range of coaching and training interventions on the topics listed above, especially in the context of strategy definition, change management design and implementation, cost reduction exercises, and enhanced customer service programs.

Laura is a Professional Certified Coach (PCC) by the International Coach Federation (ICF) and Certified Professional Co-Active Coach (CPCC). She is currently taking the ORSC course (Organization and Relationship Systems Coaching) and works in English, French, Spanish and Catalan.

Special thanks to...

- Laura for leading this Pluribus book project! With your drive and organization, you were able to coordinate a book with 13 different authors from all over the world, well done!

- Rohini for your beautiful and inspiring foreword. It gives all of us a lot of energy and motivation to foster the D&I journey in our personal and professional lives

- Each single writer of this book for being part of our Pluribus adventure and sharing your passion and experience with us

- Jean-Michel, Bonnie, José, Lena, Tim, Amel and Sue for your precious inputs, feedback or words of encouragement while reading the various drafts of the book

- Raphael and Sarah for your continuous support and love and also for your great help with some translations and editing

- The entire Pluribus network who hold us together with positive energy throughout the whole process

- Our families, friends, colleagues and clients for your incredible and moving testimonials you sent us! What a privilege to have you in our lives

- Mindy and her team for leading us through the writing, editing and designing processes from A to Z

Testimonials

"Over a time period of almost 10 years, and from the very beginning the success of our collaboration has been based on a strong trusting partnership with the shared vision, with the same passion and mindset! I want to thank Isabelle and the Pluribus team for sharing your wisdom and accompanying Sodexo and me to grow during this rich D&I journey."

Satu Heschung, VP of Global Diversity and Inclusion, Sodexo

"Isabelle founded Pluribus when she left BP and what an amazing journey the last ten years has been for Isabelle and Pluribus. The core offer of valuing and embracing diversity and inclusion is held strongly as a value and genuinely practiced by Isabelle and all the faculty, most of whom I've had the privilege to work with and value as my friends. Pluribus is synonymous with Isabelle — inspiring, courageous, committed and passionate to make a difference by supporting organizations to maximize the potential of their diverse workforce and improve business performance and results."

Linda Murray - Senior Vice President of Global HR, Singapore

"Great experience with Isabelle and Pluribus. We worked together to build our first international Diversity & Inclusion meeting with colleagues joining from all around the world. A lot of energy, deep thinking, reflection and actions to further move the D&I agenda at Sanofi."

Paul Waltmann - Diversity Head, Human Resources, Sanofi

"In the past years, Pluribus has been a great contributor in creating awareness on the importance of bias in our organization."

Sonia Studer - Global Head of Diversity & Inclusion, Nestlé

"I have been an Associate and friend of Pluribus for the last eight years and have welcomed both the variety of opportunities (U.K., France, Belgium, USA, Dubai, Tokyo, Bangkok, Indonesia, China) and the close cooperation and support of the gifted Pluribus community. The Pluribus Associate model is the blueprint for how all companies will operate in the future – diverse, open, flexible, inclusive, accountable. We model what our clients aspire to."

Nicola Shearer - Executive Coach

"I was working with Pluribus as part of an internship for one year as a junior consultant. It was such a fascinating and growing experience for me because I was able to get insights on how diversity and inclusion can completely metamorphose the vision and values of corporations and how it can have a positive impact on businesses on a professional and personal level. The human interactions, workshops and group exercises that I was a part of helped me develop my own awareness on the importance of inclusion in such a diverse world. I also learned the various approaches to good communication and feedback in a team and it will surely help me grow in my new job, so that I can lead by example and become a good manager. I am truly grateful for this amazing experience and cannot wait to be involved again later down the line with Pluribus!"

Raphael Pujol - Artist and Repertoire Manager

"Pluribus is doing more than just accelerating the Diversity & Inclusion agenda in the corporate world. Pluribus is a true family. Isabelle and her team welcome you (literally at home!), share their life experience and are genuinely committed to guide you through your diversity and inclusion journey. They support you with their passion and willingness to make a stand to challenge the status quo."

Stéphanie Oueda Cruz

"It has been and continues to be a wonderful experience collaborating with everyone at Pluribus. I am so proud to partner with a team of passionate and dedicated colleagues whose vision is to create safe spaces where men and women raise their self-awareness by engaging in transparent dialogue leading to intentional inclusion. I appreciate the opportunity to facilitate personal growth and full self-realization."

Jose R. Cox - Facilitator

"L'Oréal started working with Pluribus almost 10 years ago when Isabelle Pujol helped the Group to define the new Diversity strategy. Since then Pluribus has been one of the main external partners to help L'Oréal with the conceptualization and roll-out of the Diversity workshop: a one-day mandatory training for all of our employees. Today Pluribus associates from all over the world help our teams to train our employees. We are very thankful to have such a competent, reliable and experienced partner at our side and wish the whole Pluribus team a lot of success for the next 10 years."

Marie-Aude Torres Maguedano -
International Diversity & Inclusion Director, L'Oréal

"I have been part of the Pluribus network for two main reasons. The first one is about values: I believe that the work of helping ourselves see beyond the surface of differences that exist so that they can embrace both the commonality that connects all people AND the uniqueness that each of us brings is key to our evolution as people, as communities, as humans. And doing this sort of work with colleagues who share these values makes the work that much more generative. The second one is about friendship and inspiration: Isabelle, as the founder and guiding force at the heart of the Pluribus network of practitioners is a true visionary, a woman whose heart is open and welcoming, and a leader who is able to engage, envision and inspire her friends, colleagues and clients. I am lucky to be her friend and colleague. And my life is simply richer as a result."

Dorian-Patrizia Baroni - Executive Coach

"Putting into words such a magical and blessed relationship that has developed in the last year is not an easy task. Pluribus supported the development of the Beyond Bias program for Hilti to be implemented globally and as I started our D&I journey in Hilti North America it became clear that a more inclusive approach would be needed within our organization. By combining the content and expertise from Pluribus with Our Culture Journey, we would be embedding D&I within our culture. What evolved since that decision is a reflection of a special group of individuals guided by the sole desire to impact and improve our workforce. Isabelle and her team of facilitators have absolutely understood our organizational culture and have been instrumental in bringing awareness to the importance of inclusion. It has been such a success that our CEO has requested that all team members continue the journey with support from Pluribus and not internal trainers. The most amazing commonality with the D&I community is the willingness to help by listening and sharing experiences. Here is where Isabelle lives the saying: "Giving without expecting anything in return." I feel that Pluribus' success is a reflection of Isabelle's selfless guidance and willingness to connect with people and enable networking among practitioners. After all, we know that engagement and best results come out of being inclusive! I envision our relationship developing in many dimensions because the personal connection is a gift!"

**Silvia Siqueira - Diversity & Inclusion Senior Manager,
Hilti North America**

"Diversity & Inclusion is so much about building bridges — thank you Isabelle for supporting us in doing so!"

Julia Hillbrandt - HR Business Partner, Hilti

"From the moment I met Isabelle I knew that someone very special had entered my life. As authentic as they come, Isabelle's ability to really see people is a rare and precious gift, rivaled only by her keen level of self-awareness. Collaborating with Isabelle, who exhibits compassion and courage with equal ease, is like being held by strong and loving arms. My life has been enriched by Isabelle's presence and I feel lucky to be sharing this journey together."

Michele Steckler - Founder, Fly Loft

"As we were rather late to address diversity and inclusion, we had the luxury to learn from best practice. We therefore teamed up with Isabelle Pujol to create and deliver awareness trainings. Isabelle made a difference with her huge experience and the way she challenged us and our top leaders. She created curiosity and hunger for more. The best start you could have on a D&I journey."

Eivind Slaan - Head of People & Culture Development, Hilti

"A very big thank you to a ladybird called Isabelle Pujol. In my position of Global Head of Diversity for BNP Paribas and even now in my new position, a meeting or a conference with Pluribus is always a great time: professionalism, caring, open eyes, mind and heart, all this in the name of diversity and respect. Good flight to the ladybird!"

Elisabeth Karako - BNP Paribas

"I was 13 when the company was created. It goes without saying that I grew up alongside Pluribus, and I was privileged to see it blossom into an inspirational, pertinent and stimulating company throughout the years. During my adolescence, Pluribus continually influenced me and has molded me into the open-minded, multicultural and respectful woman I am today, just as much for my professional life as for my personal!"

Sarah Pujol - Freelance Stage Manager

"I never knew the true meaning and importance of diversity and inclusion till I moved away from Africa to Europe working for major multinationals. I always assumed that all human being were the same and we should be treated and given the same opportunities in life to thrive and make our mark in this world. However, working for the first time in a multicultural context, I discovered how naïve I was and how complex it was to lead, communicate, manage relationships, and make decisions in a multicultural context. Having experienced first-hand discrimination (unintentional) and seeing the impact it had on my self-confidence and my performance, I made my intention and my goal to work hard and do my utmost to raise awareness about difference and the values from it. As Isabelle always says, inclusion is a choice and a personal choice, so if you want to tap into people's potential and access a different level of intelligence and innovation, we need, as organizations and individuals, to invest in upskilling our people and our leaders to lead communities rather than just organizations.

Diversity & Inclusion is also beyond just being a course, it is a collective ongoing journey."

Amel Murphy - Co-founder of Sustain Leadership and Senior Pluribus Associate for the Middle East Region

"I met Isabelle 26 years ago. I consider her as a colleague and a friend. From the beginning, I have been impressed by her determination to achieve her goals, by her sincerity and her empathy for others. She is strongly embedding the Diversity & Inclusion values in her daily life!

Thanks Isa to continue your way next to me."

Micheline Ruelle - Pluribus D&I Coordinator

"Ten years with Pluribus means for me ten years with a deep relationship to Isabelle who is passionate to attract, develop and retain talents, because Isabelle was my line manager before she founded Pluribus.

What do I want to share with you? In 2002 during the integration of BP, Veba Oel and Castrol in Germany, my HR manager encouraged me to apply for a job in Diversity & Inclusion (D&I), at that time a completely unknown function. It was a strange approach as he said: "There is a French woman, speaking English and working on a topic I have never heard before: D&I. As you are open to new challenges I would appreciate if you would apply for a job in D&I." I was interested to get more information on D&I and to learn how the new organization which changed from a traditional German to a non-traditional English company ticks. So I applied for the job. It was my first interview in English – and the worst performance I ever had. I was not authentic, had no self-confidence, because my English was not as eloquent as my German and my examples to show my competencies were not powerful. Isabelle noticed that, gave me space to relax and asked for my hobby. Immediately I felt better and talked with excitement about dancing Tango Argentino. Suddenly I was not self-conscious of speaking English, I showed my enthusiasm for this wonderful dance and all the countries where the Tango has led me to. Isabelle directly felt my deep passion for Tango Argentino and decided: If this person is so passionate about a hobby, I will try to build this passion for D&I. And she did!

She was an inspiring leader, gave me self-confidence to grow in an international environment and supported me to develop my skills and competencies. It was a unique experience to work with and learn from her. And she was successful: today I am the D&I Manager for Fuels in Europe and Southern Africa. Thank you Isabelle, that you believed in me and gave me the chance to grow. Hopefully some time we will again have the chance to work together and to support others when they want to attract, develop and retain their talents across the world."

Dorothee Vogt - Diversity & Inclusion Manager for Fuels, Europe & Southern Africa, BP

"Living this precious one life we have for almost half a century,
I have been thinking that I had quite an eclectic working life so far.
Looking back though, being included/excluded and its impact on every
single being including myself seems a golden thread of interest for
me. Working with Isabelle, all my colleagues at Pluribus and all our
clients, I feel very lucky and humbled to have the chance to look closer
at this very human need; to explore and to hone our skills together for
this small step for men and women and giant leap for our world."

Nükhet Solak - Senior Associate, Pluribus

"When Isa told me some ten years ago that she was to start Pluribus I
thought that it was a very strategic thing to do, but I was not surprised.
Isabelle had been at the forefront of the Diversity & Inclusion agenda
for years and her vision of a business where she could 'drop in,'
diagnose issues with its culture and work with individuals at all levels
to come up with their tailored solutions was and remains correct.
Isabelle and the Pluribus team are savvy operators, living up to the
strategic rationale that started it all."

Marcelo Cardoso - Group Head of Compliance,
Petrofac Limited

"Isabelle Pujol is a shining blend of intelligence, open-heartedness,
integrity, courage and commitment to the human potential in each of us.
In a precarious time on this planet when factions are pitted against one
another she believes that there is no "other." I count her as a precious
friend and inspiring colleague."

Barbara Cecil, Author, *Coming Into Your Own, a Woman's Guide*
Through Life Transitions

"Beyond her passion and professionalism, listening is Isabelle's great quality. Every time we have worked together, she understood our needs perfectly and found limpid solutions to questions such as: 'How to build a diversity roadmap' and 'How to raise awareness through our Diversity Council all over the world.' Let's continue your road!"

Laurence Reckford - Diversity Department Manager, Total

"I first reached out to Isabelle after a network referral as I was looking for a partner for some work at Cargill. As often happens, we were working to a tight deadline and in a matter of an hour created a bond that has expanded far beyond the professional realm. That first encounter has been the foundation of a multi-year friendship. Isabelle is a friend, coach and development partner – we share similar values and beliefs in life. She truly lives and breathes the spirit of inclusion in all her activities and encounters."

Maija Van Langendonck

"Active listening, goodwill and kindness, empathy… Isabelle Pujol has these great human qualities that enable people to speak freely and trust each other. Let's get inspired by her."

Mathilde Tabary, D&I Manager, Carrefour